BEYOND THE ICEBERG

BEYOND
THE
ICEBERG

A Case for Emotional Healing

CHRISTIANA ONU, PhD

Beyond the Iceberg
A Case for Emotional Healing

iUniverse books may be ordered through booksellers or by contacting:

iUniverse
1663 Liberty Drive
Bloomington, IN 47403
www.iuniverse.com
844-349-9409

ISBN: 978-1-4759-5190-5 (sc)
ISBN: 978-1-4759-5191-2 (hc)
ISBN: 978-1-4759-5192-9 (e)

Library of Congress Control Number: 2012917904

Print information available on the last page.

iUniverse rev. date: 10/18/2023

DEDICATION

This book is dedicated to men and women of good nurture, who are constantly fighting for the success and advancement of other people. In the words of my loving husband, "He who keeps honest relationship is always very close to God."

PROMOTIONAL BLURBS

This is great, Dr. Christiana Onu. I had the privilege of witnessing your wonderful performances at your PhD Defense in New York and reading through your Dissertation, which has metamorphosed into a book of Counseling Psychology. I strongly believe that the taste of the pudding is in the eating. I will urge people to get a copy of this book today and testify to themselves that Dr. Onu has made an enormous contribution to the field of education and life in general.

Rev. Barrister Anthony Ezeoke
Author, "The Catholic Priesthood: Recapturing the Fading Glory".

* * * *

Congratulations my daughter, Dr. Christy! I have always paused and wondered at your humility and intelligence. I was highly delighted to go through your life enriching book. This is a panacea, a 21st Century Pain Reliever. Reading through your book gives me such an indescribable joy that a married woman could go into an extensive research like this, to guide humanity towards the path of longevity, the Devine and therapeutic healing which society so badly needs now. I am proud of you, worthy daughter.

Ugoeze (Dr.) Josephine Nwachukwu Udaku,
K.S.M, JP, M.F.R., Former President, National Catholic Women Organization of Nigeria (NCCWO).

*   *   *   *

The scholarship of this book anchors on Dr. Christiana Onu's creative intelligence, experience and professionalism to visualize a situation that is completely not there, carried out a research on it and contextually developed a powerful academic study on a woman and her two children who seem to have been devastated by sickness and life threatening conditions. After reading through that section of her book, I was stampeded to underline how productive this book is to society and individuals in their various emotional problems and needs.

Rev. Dr. Kevin A. Iwuoha, Pastor, Holy Trinity Parish, Arroyo, Seco, New Mexico, USA

*   *   *   *

I highly recommend this book to all and sundry. It is really fascinating and therapeutic.

Dr. Slate Stphen,
Executive Director, Institute of Mediation and Conflict Resolution Center, NY

TABLE OF CONTENTS

PREFACE

*"Have we ever been more concerned about those who upset,
curse and hurt us than we are concerned about ourselves?"*
- Prof. Nwachukwu A. O.

The above question, for me, summarizes the relevance of this book. I posited it in the first place because after I finished reading Dr. Christiana Onu's manuscript, I pin-pointed why this book should generally become a hand book for counseling psychology. Naturally, we are inclined to think, emphasize and care only for ourselves, our security and safety more than we think or care for others. Nobody is an island. We need each other for life to be more meaningful. While there is absolute need for each of us to take proper care of him or herself, we should not be askant or disinterested in the needs and progress of other people. Cyclically, we get solutions to our problems when we first take care of other people's concerns. The message of this book "Beyond the ice berg" presupposes the fact that there are so many problems people have which are physically not noticeable. These are the problems that influence their actions.

We easily react to sense knowledge than what is deeply-rooted in the heart and this is the awareness the author is creating in this book. For instance, if your partner or a friend unexpectedly yells at you, what normally should be your first reaction? Of course, we do not take such insults lightly but hit back immediately. But, is there any gain or point engaging in a fight with somebody you have not walked in his shoes? People carry heavy burdens and at times get blinded by worries and melancholy. Most often, we blame people we should sympathize with, and that is why I consider this book timely and urgent. If society should begin to realize that to err is human but persistence in error is diabolical, life should be more appreciated and livable. In other words, when we appreciate one another in the little things we do for, and soft words we speak to them, healing occurs.

Undoubtedly, here lies the irreplaceable role of psychological practice which this book has systematically and succinctly addressed. Once we are aware of a particular danger or obstacle in our relationships or lives, navigating through or conquering it becomes easier. Such awareness is important in dealing with our natural splinters, the ice-burg that may keep us constantly upset or sad. There are times, moments we do not feel good. The awareness that living, allowing or prolonging our unhealthy moments leads to so many psychological hazards, places us on the right path to seek peace and create joy for ourselves, come what, come may. Here again scores and underlines the classic need for this book.

Eventually, the general overview of this undertaking or book is an incorporation of Psychology and Practice in approaching some of the major problems facing individuals today such as emotional, physical, socio-religious etc, that are not manifested outwardly. The practical application of the value of psychology to human life cannot be overemphasized today, especially considering the difficulties many go through in their lives. Hence, the need for counseling becomes urgent and important. It is not enough to study the emotional problems of people without finding a way to address them. Yet, to address them, one needs to find out the cause of the problems. There is urgent need also to study and find ways to solve or tackle these problems from psychological and pastoral perspectives. There are various branches of psychology that handle one aspect of human life or the other. While this book did not claim a holistic coverage and study of all branches of psychology as such, it saliently and objectively examined those applied branches of psychology that deal with specific areas of human needs. One of these applied types includes counseling psychology, which addresses the needs of individuals in their various emotional problems that seem to constitute obstacles in their everyday living.

Generally, psychology appears to be at the center of human life and dynamism involving the way one thinks, feels, behaves and acts. There are so many theories in psychology that need to be tested and put into action. In this book, the author reviewed the works of some famous psychologists, psychoanalyst, psychotherapists and what have you, as ways to achieve her set objectives. These are personalities and experts whose contributions in the field of psychological practice could assist society move forward in the right direction. Luckily, her specialty as a nurse coupled with her rigorous studies and research at Graduate Theological Foundation, Indiana, led the author to conclude that human beings deserve the best treatment and attention on the planet due primarily to their complex nature.

In her Master's Degree from the same Institution, the author attempted to approach the issue of psychology from pastoral perspectives, in which she isolated human problems within a larger context to underline the enormity and ocean of differences in the various plights that plague society and individuals. In other words, the author tried to distinguish to what extent psychology could be applied in the various pastoral problems people face in their daily lives. For instance, asking a person who is deaf and dump from birth to sing unto the Lord is a form of mockery and ridicule to God.

Unfortunately, some of us tend to limit pastoral studies within the ambiance of Church-related activities. But this book has revealed that pastoral psychology goes beyond the confines of the Church to areas of need that have nothing to do with religion in the first place. Reaching out to others in their miseries with supportive presence and compassion is a form of pastoral care that knows no boundaries. It does not matter who needs our support - an Atheist, a Minister of the Gospel, a Pagan, a Hindu etc, it makes no difference. For instance, a domestic case involving couples or people who have no religion calls for Mediation, Counseling or Pastoral Psychology. In such situations, the Pastoral or counseling Psychologist is bound to offer professional assistance to such people irrespective of their religious affiliations.

It is necessary to note that counseling psychology as a profession is equally pastoral from a technical perspective. These differences Dr. Onu clarified in her book. However, the emphasis in this book is on Counseling Psychology which is the author's area of concentration and specialty. In terms of area of intended service, the book is all embracing, laudable and holistic. In a matter like this, there is every need to note what the Book of Isaiah documented here:

> *I am he who says of Cyrus, 'My shepherd- he will fulfill my whole purpose, saying of Jerusalem, "Let her be rebuilt", and of the Temple, "Let your foundation be laid". Thus says Yahweh to his anointed, to Cyrus, whom he has taken by his right hand to subdue nations before him and strip the loins of kings, to force gateways before him that their gates be closed no more (Isaiah 44: 28; 45: 1).*

From the above quotation, we can vividly discover that counseling or pastoral psychology extends to every stratum of individual lives and society. God knew that Cyrus was a pagan king of the Persians.

He also knew that this king did not believe in him or worship him. Yet, God single handedly picked him to deliver his people from exile in Babylon. Not only did God choose him for this prophetic mission, but he also addressed a pagan king as "My shepherd, my anointed, who would fulfill his purpose". Comparatively, the point is that God has no favorite, anybody who obeys him, from any nationality, is acceptable to him. God knew there was a pastoral need for his people in bondage and decided to deliver them through a pagan king. Similarly, this was the passion that drove the author into this area of study. Thus, she has demonstrated her pastoral zeal, not only as a Counselor and Psychologist, but also Pastoral Care giver.

Consequently, we can deduce from the above biblical citation how pastoral psychology utilizes psychological tools for its operation. It was doubtless that the people in exile were frustrated, emotionally wounded, and had great need for deliverance from their misery and melancholy. Hence, God appointed a pagan king, Cyrus for that purpose. Besides, the destruction of their Temple in Jerusalem was the most humiliating event in the lives of the Israelites that called for immediate attention. This is where I believe that "events" are stages upon which certain people build and change the world. The 'certain people" mentioned here has no reference to any ethnic group, race or language. As it were, God did not consider the issue of religion an option in saving his people or more important than the mission he expected his anointed one to accomplish for his people.

Psychologically, we can imagine the effect of this accomplished mission in the lives of the chosen race. That is the aim of pastoral psychology, to bring life to those who have lost hope as a result of one striking event, devastation, misery or the other. In this instance, counseling psychology takes its course. When we speak of "Beyond the ice berg", it is all about the value of psychology in the hidden lives of society, a case for healing or counseling and the basic needs of individuals, in terms of their stressful stages and moments. In a practical language, psychology provides the skills and tools for counseling and this is precisely what Dr. Onu has applied in this book.

According to one of my remarks, "For instance, frustration levels tend to be unbearably high in relationships where and when partners claim to be right and just in whatever they do" (Nwachukwu, 2010:162). In actual fact, in counseling, the counselor tries to examine the splinters, electricity of feelings and why these partners claim to be right in whatever they do, even when their actions and behaviors are contradictorily against common sense and societal values. Something must be responsible for such resilient dominance in individual actions or points of view. Help can only be possible when the counselor has found out the main reasons and root causes of the conflicting positions that create stress or frustration for the said partners in our context.

Ineluctably, one of the greatest problems that confront society today is not how one feels at the mountain top experiences but what is accomplished or achieved at the valley of every day experiences. Technically, the author has handled these problems in professional manners. We have so many psychologists who lack sensitivity to the problems facing society. The same ugly practice happens among religious leaders. Many preachers of the Gospel message, at times, mount the pulpit and announce the message of hope, restoration, and favors without even caring to study and understand the nature of problems individuals experience in their lives. Nominally, it is easier and one thing to console bereaved family members and another to assist them cope with their grief.

Blaming young people for indiscipline is only proper and genuine if they have ever been schooled and cultured in sound moral lives. A person with impaired or listening disability can only be blamed for keeping silence if he had heard the instructions properly in the first place. That is why the issue of spirituality cannot be excogitated from counseling. People behave the ways they are and the levels of individual actions or behaviors point to their spiritual contents. Thus, the author is concerned, not so much with what people do as the reasons behind such actions. Counseling is more of a spiritual exercise than religious. Any person who engages in one form of activity or the other is spiritual irrespective of his or her religion. No wonder, Thayer in support of the study of spiritual psychology, remarked:

In the most general sense, spirituality has to do with how we experience ourselves in relation to what we designate as the source of the ultimate power and meaning in life, and how we live out that relationship. Spirituality is not merely feelings; it has to do with the integration and coherence of ourselves as experiencing and acting persons (Thayer in Nwachukwu, 2010:164; Vision, NACC, Oct. 2007:5).

There are so many things that sound little in the eyes of the world that constitute great harm to society generally. This is the point Dr. Onu would want her readers to underline in this book. Just as Nwachukwu once expressed it:

These 'experiencing' and 'acting' aspects of human life provide the backgrounds and bones on which spiritual psychology anchors and builds its analysis and operations. These operations include how a child strives and imbibes societal values in its personality developmental stage and how these values later shape and inform its character in life (Ibid).

Some people who have no idea of the academic target, intensity and challenges, which are being advanced at Graduate Theological

Foundation, Indiana, an affiliate of Oxford University, England, may not appreciate the enormity of work accomplished there. For instance, this book is the fruit of such challenges. While some prospective candidates get preoccupied by certain logistics as whether the Institution is accredited, recognized or can fetch one a nice job in the market industry, many who availed themselves of the educational opportunities from there, have ever proven productive, both on the educational levels and other ministries. As it were, the knowledge this book offers society and as based on some textbooks of outstanding authors on psychological practices is the springboard and high water mark of this book. As a counselor, the author has availed society and individuals with the vital information and healing opportunity they need to deal with some of the emotional problems in life.

Therefore, I strongly recommend this book to individuals, support group members, families, therapists, organizations, the school systems, both secondary and tertiary, etc, that battle with one psychological problem or the other. It is my belief that people can change. This book offers them the skills and language to understand themselves and take decision for healthier living opportunities. The only way to achieve the fruit of this undertaking is by grabbing your own copy today and read it. The language is very simple and clear.

Fr. Anthony O. Nwachukwu, Ph.D, Psy.D,
Prof. of Counseling Psychology and West African Studies,
Faculty Consultant, Bureau of West African Scholars.
www.gtfeducation.org

ACKNOWLEDGMENT

First and foremost, I must unflinchingly express deep gratitude to God, Almighty. "Lord, I thank You, for You are wonderful indeed. You knew I would not have made it without You. I remembered when I nearly lost hope in undertaking such an uphill task. With family responsibilities and workload, I thought I could not make it but You stood by and accompanied me all the way till now. Thank You for being there for me and always reaching down to rescue and assist me in times of great need. I love You".

I am singularly indebted to all those who have assisted me through this educational journey, especially, those authors, experts, and professionals, whose books, skills and materials have been utilized and quoted in the development of this book. In this light, my heartfelt appreciations go to my experienced and hardworking Supervisor, Prof. Anthony O. Nwachukwu, for his technical, skillful guidance and for working day and night to see that this monograph meets academic requirements for the Award of a Ph.D Degree in Counseling Psychology. God bless you.

I sincerely thank my Mom, Lolo Regina Ekeh for her encouragement, support and prayers during the course of my studies at GTF. You are the best Mom, especially for sowing in all of us, those seeds and values of right choices and behaviors. Mama, thank you so much.

On a special note, I thank my Dad, Late Sir/Chief Celestine Uwazie Onuoha Ekeh for inculcating in his children the spirit of hard work and for his insistence that "education and good life are the vehicles to success". I know you are with the Lord; I still appreciate your prayers. I miss you every single day.

On a very special way, my greatest thanks go to my life partner and husband, our children, my sisters and brothers for being there for me. I cannot thank you enough.

My unalloyed appreciations go to the members of the Staff of GTF, especially, The Academic Affairs Committee, Registrar, Provost, Directors of various academic functions, Alumni, Fellow Grandaunts, The Dean and School of Graduate Admissions, and more especially, The President, Dr. John H. Morgan for your heroic role in setting up for the human race, a wonderful and unique educational system that gradually transforms people in a meaningful manner. I will ever remain grateful to God for graduating from this practically oriented and 21st Century Institution, GTF, Affiliate of Oxford University, London and Centro Pro Unione, Rome.

Finally, there are friends and acquaintances especially at my work place, in Nigeria and in the United States, whose names ought to be mentioned here, besides those who wish to remain anonymous, I ask of your pardon and pray God to bless each and every one of you for your assistance during this time-consuming and intellectual journey. I appreciate your enormous and immense contributions.

INTRODUCTION

"There is no art to find man's construction in the face"
(Shakespeare's Macbeth: Act 1, scene 4).

It is important to set the record straight ab initio. This book explores the value of psychology as a necessary tool to deal with and understand human behaviors and problems for interpersonal relationships and healthy living. My area of research or concentration being on Counseling Psychology, it is my utmost concern to systematically utilize the tools it offers to the benefit of society and individuals in their emotional plights. Studies have proved that, sometimes, we point accusing fingers to others on ugly habits and issues we create ourselves. The worst sickness any person can suffer from is 'hypochondria' – feeling of being sick when there is none or insecure when there is full security. Each of us is his or her own story and reality. We are perceived as stories and these stories eventually define who we are as human beings.

When Shakespeare wrote, he specifically understood the dynamics of life as being cyclical. For instance, a person who appears or dresses funny in a gathering may be the most intelligent among the group. At times, we claim to have answers to non-existent issues or feel guilty when no offences have been committed, even when we have not been accused. There are so many things that happen in our lives that defile the surface. We tend to deal with external stimuli and feel normal that everything is okay, when, in actual fact, perception may not have the complete story.

At times, many of us are wired to believing that our values as human beings depend on others' estimations and judgments, when, in actual fact, they are simply guessing or speculating. Only the individual knows himself. For instance, in a family where one of the partners is dishonest, the only way he or she puts up with guilt is by making nasty remarks, name-calling, and unnecessarily pointing an accusing finger to the one who holds the peace of the family. At times, we get angry, hurt and upset over such ugly behaviors without even knowing that he or she needs a professional help. This is precisely why people do not change their silly behaviors because we pointed them out - their mistakes and faults. In the same par, people do not love us because we are readily there to give them advices. Reality differs. That you like something does not make or mean it is right and being delighted in a particular menu does not make it healthy. My reality as a Counselor is the sum total of my personal thoughts which may be positive or negative, and different from those of other people.

Each of us takes the limits of his or her own level and field of perception or vision. There is no point passing judgments on those we have not walked in their shoes or understood their worldviews. This is where Prof. Anthony O. Nwachukwu's dictum comes true, "Nobody is insignificant" (Nwachukwu, 2011). People have the potentials to make differences in their lives and the ability to transform their environments. When you begin to perceive others as fools, you might be the fool in question, because, it is more of matching on your own drum beat. Therefore, it is baseless picking quarrel with a person who does not have the correct information as you do or is not sound upstairs.

Consequently, "We don't see things the way they are but as we are" [Thinkexist.com] because "we perceive stimuli that impinge upon our senses....Perception", though positive, "constructs rather than records 'reality" – [Michael Michalko, November 13, 2011]. The popular aphorism that appearances deceive is very true considering the complex being we call 'human'. There are so many questions I have raised in this book that still remain unanswered. I have no slightest doubt in my mind that there is mysterious Being, God who created man in his own image. Thus, man is a mystery too. But, whenever I begin to wonder at the beauty and mystery of creation, I cannot come to conclusive terms or grasp the magnitude of God's resemblance with humanity. Many people go through a lot of traumas due primarily to disappointments and frustrations in their lives.

If man is created in God's image, to what extent does human conditions, misery, suffering, melancholy, grief, pain etc., reflect in God? Studies have revealed that each person behaves true to type. It then follows that there must be a universal image of God which an individual shares with him. Therefore, the various attributes of a bad person cannot be ascribed to God, who is totally holy. For man to share any identity or image with God, he has to put up such values as goodness, steadfastness, truth, justice and love for God and one another.

The need for "Counseling Psychology" which is the focus of my PhD Degree Program at GTF cannot be over emphasized today. As noted in my opening statement, the thrust of this book is to utilize the values of psychology and practice in dealing with peoples' problems in the moment. The need for psychology and its classic importance or uniqueness in human lives has to be given an academic attention. Most often, some people are confronted with psychological problems they do not know their sources. At times, they know the sources whereas others do not. Even, in a situation where the sufferer knows and others know too, provision of services and skills to deal with such psychological issues may not be forthcoming or there.

Therefore, it is important to create this awareness so that people may begin to expect the unexpected in others' behaviors. We talk of and react to our conscious lives and may not know of the subconscious. This is primarily why I pressed on with this undertaking. I want to be part of the healing processes of my people and those who might need my expertise in their individual cases too. For instance, a lot of things happen unexpectedly. Couples quarrel over trivial matters; marriages go into flames, responsibilities abandoned, etc. because of lack of informed consent or the correct information. It is also my dream that after people have read this book, they will be able to arm themselves with the information that can guide their relationships with others.

As I said already, there are many incapacitations due to sickness, bad associations, accident or ignorance etc. Good families break into pieces, friendships go to blazes or into flames, some people take to drug addictions, alcoholism, teenagers join band groups and companies and good lives are being destroyed on daily basis on account of the above reasons. Therefore, the earlier we begin to self-supervise our behaviors in relations to how we view and perceive others, the better for society and individuals.

Besides, there are so many emotional problems among us that have not been perceived and addressed. Or do we expect everybody to come to the hospital for attention, even for hunger? Thus, I feel obliged to do something to rescue the situation at hand and make my own contributions towards some levels of alleviations, hence the choice of my topic. Besides being a nurse and mother, I still have the burning zeal and urge to serve humanity for the sake of the love of God and man.

In this manner, I shall incorporate my Mission Statement here; call it, "The Purpose of the Study" which focuses on the same academic goal to buttress my points in this book also. Therefore, this prologue shall equally serve as a resume of what we expect to read from the book. Psychology is human and concerns every living thing. But professional counseling falls within the realm of rational human beings who are skillfully equipped to assist fellow human beings in need, especially those needs we do not normally know about.

Interestingly, most of my family members entered medical and pharmaceutical schools and graduated as doctors and pharmacists. My husband is also a pharmacist by profession and owns his own pharmaceutical company. Along the same perspective, I felt that my calling was in the nursing profession, so that I could, at close contacts, assist humanity in a more practical manner. I have the belief that my passion and role as a nurse should not be limited to the hospital settings only. I need to acquire the professional skills that will assist me realize my goal in this field because as already noted, I feel the need to apply my profession to the service of every one irrespective of creed, race, language and gender etc. I take it upon myself to educate, comfort, and care, not only for patients at the hospital but also to reach out for individuals and persons who have nobody to care for them, the homeless, dejected, poor, particularly our teenage boys and girls who seem to have been blown away by the wind and spirit of materialism and modernism. Listening to their inner feelings and hurt will go a long way to transform society. My book is a call to restorative justice where the offenders and their victims are given the opportunity to discuss their splinters for smoother co-habitation and healthy relationships.

On a more practical note, for the past seven years, I have tried to assist both the staff and patients, first of all, on the medical-surgical unit, telemetry unit, and then psychiatry unit. In my work place, some members of staff tell me their stories and the hurdles they go through in their families and relationships that require technical attention. Often times, some patients have asked me shocking questions like, "Nurse, do you think I will recover from this sickness?" I have, in many occasions, found myself dumbfounded as to the proper responses, not even answers to give them. The emphasis here may not be based on physically recovering from sickness as other dimensional concerns the sick person may have. It is only by listening beyond the spoken words of the patient that major clues manifest. Questions that fundamentally touch the human life and existence go beyond answers. Gradually, I feel these people do not really need answers to their questions but somebody or caring individuals to respond to their emotions and feelings.

In such cases, any supportive presence or reassuring response encourages these people deal with their situations. Even, in many cases, when I have not made any comment, the manner in which I approach or present myself to them seems to brightly put smiles on their faces. That has been my encouragement to pursue or engage in this program of inner restoration. As my career and interest in this cognate field proceeded, I found myself not only acquiring many new skills but also desperately wanting to extend my career to the level of Doctor of Philosophy in Counseling Psychology, with emphasis on counseling, essentially for the purpose of the Nigerian situation and educational goals. No wonder this book is the result of my PhD research and I expect it to eventually be a masterpiece in the area of psychological practice, dealing specifically with human problems and their solutions.

The fundamental question that went through my mind in the course of my study had been: "What do I plan to accomplish as a Doctor of philosophy in Psychology, especially with emphasis in Counseling at the end of my educational career at GTF?" In a general sense, I feel that this is professionally a continuation of what I am doing now, helping patients to overcome addictions, losses, anger, depression, trauma, ADHD, anxiety, and even broken relationships. I believe as a counselor and psychologist, I can engage on one –on-one relationship with my clients and accomplish great things in these areas and environments, which are often shunned by physicians and some nurses. In the final analysis, my denominational aim is to advance God's presence among his people on earth, particularly the sick, those who are seen and regarded as "nobody's" of society. I believe nobody is insignificant before God. The trend of regarding a fellow human being as nobody is the synthesis of human selfishness and invention and not divine. God who created humanity did not discriminate between them. He made them equal in terms of dignity of life, freedom to move around and to enjoy happiness. Some can be more gifted in intelligence, but all human gifts and riches are meant for the benefits of everyone else. A popular adage says that nobody is an island. Every human life or person is significant and purposeful. In this book, I examined all the possible channels that lead to the fulfillment of individual desires and aspirations. That is the goal of counseling.

On a personal level, my favorite activities are bicycling, reading, playing volley, and basketballs. I enjoy all outdoor sports and group activities and I will always encourage others to keep fit by engaging themselves in one workout activity or the other. Thanks to God, my family lives with me in Lansdale, Pennsylvania, and it is not only a source of support for me, but also very therapeutic. We are highly religious people, ever supportive of the Church and the less privileged of society.

I look forward to beginning this new aspect of my psychological career into the doorsteps of individuals I meet and interact with. More importantly, my future employers and some of my current staff, patients and their families are anxious for me to begin practicing as a Counselor. I hope to be greatly beneficial to society and individuals by my profession in this area of hope and healing. As God would have it, Dr. Anthony O. Nwachukwu, a renowned spiritual psychologist and who is also a Faculty of the International Institute, GTF/Oxford, is my Reference Person and Supervisor. Having introduced my book, I shall now invite you to join me examine in details, the problem of the thesis in chapter one of this book.

CHAPTER ONE

<span style="text-align:center">~~~</span>

THE STATEMENT OF PROBLEM

We speak of the values of psychology for the advancements of society and the individual because something has necessitated them. There are problems in society that need to be addressed or fixed as our introduction inferred. These are not problems for the law courts or government. They are really human problems that affect both the affective and cognitive faculties of the person. Then, our thesis statement is, "Can the values of psychology address people in their various situations and assist them come to terms with their life's huddles and obstacles?" Thus, the entire research work or book is designed to prove the above hypothesis. The human problems envisaged here and the hypothesis were approached and examined through certain criteria, the parameters, namely; "Background of study, Purpose of study, Scope of study and Significance of study". We shall try to examine these parameters separately in the same order in which they are presented. For prospective students or researchers who engage in one scientific investigation or the other, this book serves as a panacea to their educational hurdles.

Background of study

The background of any research work or book of this nature raises certain basic questions depending on the matter being discussed such as, "Have there been human situations that demanded professional attention, and were left unattended to as a result of the failure to diagnose them? Speaking of the value of psychology in dealing with human situations, has there been any time psychology was not considered in the life of the people? What has psychology got to do with a religionist, Christian or traditionalist? Is it possible that some people may be dying in silence because of the psychological problems others do not know about, even the medical personnel?" There are thousand and one questions that can be raised today as regards the value of psychology in human lives. For instance, right from my early life experiences in my country, Nigeria, I have seen a lot of people go through excruciating pains in their families, no food to feed their children or send them to school. Again, I have seen individuals from rich and wealthy families look tattered, unhappy and melancholic most of the time.

Despite the fact that these are hardworking people, they cannot have ends meet. In such situations we are inclined to evaluate them based on physical statures, but their problems may not have anything to do with material things. Material things equally affect one's psychology and beings. For instance, I still remember my classmates at primary and high schools who never paid their school fees on time. Some missed classes till the time of examinations. The case of my closest friend was very touching. She was once sent home during examination period to go and get her school fees, which she never did. That prevented her from completing her education with us. What pained me most was the fact that the student was very intelligent and promising. But because of abject poverty she could not further her education. Miserably, she had no option than to get involved in early marriage. If it were today, I could not have lived to see that young girl leave school without a certificate. Matters like the ones described above influence a person's whole being also.

Similarly, I cannot forget one family in my home that found it hard to care of her family members. There was not enough food to feed, let alone to send her family members to the hospital. Unfortunately too, some of these people who had no source of livelihood died of emotional frustration, strokes or heart attack. Yet, the stories told around were that evil spirits attacked them or their enemies poisoned them. There are a lot of things I know today that seemed to be ascribed to or associated with the spirits of the dead. But my studies have revealed that malnutrition is a disease of its own. How can one expect a hungry or sick person to behave normally? Such memories, cum the knowledge I gathered from my early childhood experiences when I was told that nurses assisted people to live better lives and feel happy and coupled with my passion to assist the needy, stampeded me into the nursing profession and the publication of this book. As a grown up woman, a nurse and psychologist, I have seen the need to achieve my life aspirations, coming to the aid of those experiencing one trauma or the other. Obviously, people need to be assisted actually to have better lives or live their best lives, not only through eating and drinking, but also through a healthy life pattern that is professionally guided.

Purpose of Study
I have already given a hint on my passion for the needy. Most of these problems require a technical approach that employs skills and experiences. Thus, based on the foregoing reasons and sufferings most people go through in their lives especially in my own country and village, Ekwereazu Umuokirika, I have decided to find a way out. And the best way I have chosen is through a practical application of my expertise in the area of counseling. The need to suggest the possible ways in which individuals can cope with sufferings and assert the special people they are, as important human documents in their lives cannot be overemphasized.

This book, therefore, aims at helping people come to terms with difficulties and sufferings, bearing in mind that sufferings are part of the human lots. There will be no time on this planet when people will not experience one difficulty or the other, and at one time in their lives or the other. Difficulties come in patches; some encounter theirs in childhood, some others at school age, in business, or in married lives, etc. But when sufferings become ways of life, then something has to be done to find solutions to them and these are the purpose of this book. The more each person is resolved to deal with his or her own problems, the better for that individual. Again, the best manner an individual can assist himself in such emotional situations is to seek help from a professional or counselor who has the management strategies to address the problems from the root.

The Scope of Study
The need for psychological practice like counseling in our time is urgent and universal in nature, scope and content. Every nation under this planet wants peace and progress and the individuals who make up the nation equally aspire to maximize the beauty and peace of their environments. Hence, we speak of eco-spirituality today. Our environments are essential ingredients for good and happy living and any violation of these fundamentals of life, either through sickness or personal relationships, create unimaginable problems. From personal experiences and research, these values of peace and progress do not come as expected. Many do not seem to be bothered or feel that something is at stake when many nations or others are at wars with one another. There is corruption almost in every stratum of society, individual lives, institutions, groups, associations and companies etc. Besides, our land appears polluted by filths, dirt, sound moral erosion, and nothing looks normal again. Thus, the net result is anarchy or state of emergency where there is total disorder and disarray. An unsafe environment breeds unrest of mind which may not be easily detected by others.

Consequently, trying to apply strategies that can assist society on a global level is envisaged but it may not be realistic or feasible in a research work or book of this magnitude. Therefore, it is intended that our discussions, though of universal application, in this book will slightly be limited to a specific population, precisely my hometown, Ekwereazu Umuokirika, Imo State of Nigeria with some references to the United State of America and other countries of the world. That is to say, our main target or audience, besides other countries, is Ekwereazu Umuokirika, Imo State of Nigeria. On the choice of my topic, the "Beyond the ice-berg: A case for emotional healing" centers specifically on caring for individuals with personal and psychological issues, ranging from loss of jobs, friendships, relationships, to drug addictions, alcoholism, victims of sex abuse etc. In other words, this research or book is designed to address such issues for the total restoration and integration of the human person. While our audience is essentially limited to the people of Ekwereazu Umuokirika in Imo State, Nigeria, our findings and investigations in this work have global relevance for the entire general public. These findings can equally be useful and beneficial to people from other cultures and race.

Significance of Study
The whole aim for this book anchors on its relevance to society and individuals. There is a popular adage in my hometown that says: "Nobody ever says that his mother's soup is bad". On the contrary, the same adage is not applicable to research work because others read and evaluate it. Therefore, the significance of this work lies on its ability to achieve its primary purpose as indicated above, especially when people benefit from it. Days are gone when people separated psychology from practice or seemed to make it theoretical. We live in a world of unimaginable challenges. The earlier we understand that most of the problems that face us today can be handled with care, patience, hope in God and determination

the better for us. We must make our lives enjoyable despite the difficulties that surround us. These are the values we intend to bring across in this book once it is made available to the general public. These are the values that make this book relevant and significant.

In other words, no book is significant in the bookshelf, library, or publishing companies when it is not read. It has to be made available first and be read by people. It is only when this very material is read and put into practice that it can be educationally meaningful. In our context, the ability to implement the skills generally acquired from this book or psychology and applied to real life situation, that it becomes relevant. In a sense, our targeted point is, "Can this book address people in their various situations and assist them come to terms with their life's huddles and obstacles?" This is the target of the author or researcher and once this targeted focus is achieved, then the book becomes relevant. That is to say, the relevance of this book lies in the hands of the reader, who is equally ready to share the good news of the book with others.

CHAPTER TWO

~~~

REVIEW OF RELATED LITERATURE

The study and value of psychology are consequential to every living being, and they are so important today because they primarily and essentially hinge on human life as such. As we shall see from the review of some professionals and experts, there is psychology of almost everything an individual does under the sun. Therefore, in a work such as this, one would expect so many books on the subject. The study of psychology is as old as the study of man himself. But literature on these aspects of applied psychology and its value to society is not as numerous as one would expect. The need for psychological practice from the counseling perspective, especially with reference to specific cultural milieu is relatively new in the field of applied psychology. Besides, issues that lie beyond the physical world are very hard to decipher in concrete terms and not many authors have delved into and written books on them.

In view of this handicap or somewhat seeming difficulty, we shall study the works of some experts on applied psychology and try to examine their values and build or develop this book from there. In other words, we are investigating into the values of human life or psychology and how far these values can impact the development of the human or individual person from the point of view of counseling. It is the same thing asking if psychology is capable of addressing the emotional quagmire of individuals.

Considering the magnitude of problems some people and society face today, is there any possible way the needy, the sick, married couples, the ministers of the Gospel, those who have lost their jobs or their friendships, the traumatized, victims of sex scandals, drug abusers, alcoholics, can be assisted and delivered from spiritual and material bondages? In order to achieve these set goals or values, we have chosen to study various topics that deal on the need for psychological practice in a manner that is systematic, therapeutic, functional and rewarding. Thus, there are few basic categories or groupings we studied and considered expedient for this scientific presentation in this chapter. Each of these categories or groupings is numbered and identified from the letters "A to M", namely:

A. PSYCHOLOGY: THERAPEUTIC DYNAMICS IN THEORY AND PRACTICE

In each of these treatments, the value of psychology will be highlighted as the main thrust of the book. For instance, when I was a small girl, I used to hear so much about psychology. Later, in my school age, my elderly brother got admission to study psychology in the University. By then, he would proudly tell us that he was going to study about how to read our minds. He even claimed that with his psychology, he could tell our future and whatever any of us planned to do in his back. With such claims, I became so curious about the subject. That was the beginning of my interest in psychological related courses. In a way, I perceived psychology as being magical and I needed to acquire those magical powers too. But, when I got admission to do nursing, the first thing we did was general psychology. With my pre-conceived ideas and the impressions, which my elderly brother created for us about psychology, I discovered the truth of the matter.

Absolutely, psychology is neither magical nor supernatural as such. It has got to do with how we live and interact with one another and the world around us. It could be magical in a sense because the mood of an individual can easily suggest what one is up to. For instance, when somebody is crying, lamenting, and making loud noises, one can quickly surmise that something is amiss or has gone wrong somewhere. Bad moods elicit some sympathetic reactions from family members and friends and good ones often point to joy, peace, good news and amicable dispositions.

Therefore, in this book, I discussed psychology, its therapeutic dynamics, both in theory and practice. My guiding tools were some remarkable books I read and the academic videos I watched. While I reflected deeply on these educational materials, I equally borrowed some leaves from other sources I considered apt for the challenge at hand. On this instance, I briefly examined the content of psychology and what it meant in our context.

Meaning of Psychology
The word 'psychology' does not mean only one thing. It means different things according to the attitudes and behaviors of different people. There is psychology in all fields of human endeavor. Even, as you read this book, there is psychology either from the impression it makes on you as whether it satisfies your expectations and curiosity or not. In the nursing section, psychology may refer to the manners in which people handle their diagnosis, their reactions in the face of danger, sickness or death. Psychology has to address life in its concreteness for it to be useful in human conditions. It is the science that deals with mental processes and human behaviors.

Etymologically, it comes from two Greek words "psyche" (mind) and 'logos' meaning the study or science of the mind. In the words of one expert, "The most important aspects of human psychology are precisely those unique factors which make us human" (Prof. Daniel N. Robinson, Part 1, 1997:5). While individual characteristics differ, there are certain factors that make us human beings as Robinson has pointed out here. These unique factors include the various organs of our bodies, the physical and the internal. At times, these unique factors are not easily recognized without professional approaches and applications.

As sensible beings, we react to stimulus, the taste of food, decide whether it is tasty or not, the nature of sight we encounter, whether it is pleasant or ugly, what we hear, whether it is worth listening to or not, what we smell around us, whether they are offensive or aromatic. Also, on our motor organs, each person moves around, walks, runs, carries, picks and lifts up objects. On the emotional level, we have feelings of our environments, the ways others treat us and express how we feel about them too. Despite the fact that feelings have no banks but have to be expressed, each person's feelings are different from those of others and may constitute some riddles for them to understand, hence this publication.

More importantly, on the cognitive and intellective level, we interpret the actions of others, read, write and understand the language others speak to us and can equally communicate with them. In every communication, there exists an ocean of indifferentism as regards the implications of other people's positions and values which may not suit ours. That is why, attentive listening is recommended in every level of communication, even in dialogue. In the words of Robinson, these are the factors that make us what we are as humans. We also encounter ourselves in a variety of ways that make us humans. Communication is symbiotic in nature, whereby each party has the opportunity to understand and grow in the knowledge of other people's positions and riches.

In the same page, Robinson maintains, "What makes an event psychological is that it is the result of human goals, desires and aspirations" (Ibid). For example, the psychology of politics talks about how individuals seek to get involved in the governance of society and how the constituents react to the government when things do not work out for their benefits. There are always goals and aspirations to meet up with in every human endeavor and these activities are psychological in nature. In religion, psychology points to how worshippers or adherents of that religion apply their faith to what they believe in, and the manner in which they are able to carry that out in their lives speaks of their persons too. In religion as such, they do this to win the favor of their God. Everything on the planet seems to have its own psychology, and in one way or the other, human beings are the main beneficiaries. It is within these contexts that we can write about its therapeutic dynamics and "psychological practice" in the lives of the emotionally wounded. According to a dictionary definition, "Psychology means the science of emotions, behavior, and the mind" (Webster's Dictionary Thesaurus).

In effect, psychology involves both the sensory, cognitive, motor and emotional aspects of the human person as I noted above. It studies emotions, how people react to a particular stimulus, decisions and choices and what they think of their present and past actions. As a nurse, I have discovered that psychology substantially employs the human brain for it to function properly. The mind is the manifestation of the brain, and without the brain there is no mind or psychology. In confirmation to this claim, another source holds that "psychology is the science that deals with mental processes and behaviors or the emotional and behavioral characteristic" (The American Heritage Dictionary). These mental processes include how each person reacts to his environments, applying the various organs of the body – the senses, intellect, emotions, and how he carries out his daily activities in actuality. In a way, we are directly and indirectly challenged to study the therapeutic dynamics of psychology, within its psychological practice and the human interactive systems as they involve behaviors that create surprises and shocks to others.

Therapeutic Dynamics

By therapeutic dynamics, we are studying and applying the relevance of psychology to life itself. Every branch of human knowledge has something to offer to individuals and society in a general and particular way. In this perspective, Goot holds that "the science of psychology faces crisis" (Goot, 1987:1), once it is removed from human application or ceases to be "human science" (Ibid). The therapeutic dynamics of psychology, fundamentally point to the relevance of psychology in the first place and how it is realized in the various conditions a person finds himself. In the same argument, Frick maintains that various aspects of psychology "address our complex problems to the existential dilemmas in human experience and interpersonal relationships" (Frick, 1989:6). Let us go back to our allusions to the significance of other fields of knowledge that equally address human problems in the moment.

Practically, for instance, when we speak of politics, the first question that should pump up is, 'to what extent has politics alleviated the emotional conditions of society?' Has it always done what it is meant to do or has it failed? In the case of philosophy, though, psychology is its branch, has it ever-relieved people of the economic pains they suffer today? In the study and practice of religion, is it proper to hold that society is safer today because of religion or the hard work individuals have put up to take care of the problems that face them on daily basis? It is one thing to discuss about the therapy psychology brings in the life of a person and another how it goes about to achieving it.

The therapeutic dynamics of psychology becomes a powerful tool in the management of individual cases and problems. It is possible to hope for a rainy day at severe draught. This hope could come through or not. Some hopes create the sense of uncertainty and doubt. But, whether the hope comes through or not, the individual agent has some bases to strive ahead in the oblivion and contingencies of life. On the other hand, there are certain hopes that are more of events whose occurrences are likely to happen without doubt or with greater proximity. For instance, telling a hungry person to wait for the arrival of food items implies two things, either that the food is getting ready or the person should be ready for it. In this instance, hope is action-oriented whose fulfillment is proximate. In a sense, psychology offers the greatest hope to the hopeless of society.

On the other hand, to tell a hungry person to exercise some patience, that God would feed him, might not solve the problem at stake. Surely, God always feeds the hungry. But we are speaking of hunger here whose satisfaction is immediate. Applying the therapeutic dynamics of psychology in our own context, we can easily surmise the theoretical and practical perspectives immediately. Thus, it is necessary to discuss the theoretical aspect of the therapeutic dynamics of psychology at this point. Psychology takes care of every aspect of human action and behavior, but the ways it does that, surface in different dimensions.

Theoretical Perspectives
The word "theory" in this context is not so much concerned with principles that have no physical application. Psychology concerns life and the various ways life operates and relates. Each branch of psychology is therapeutic in the sense that it has something healing to offer to society or the individual person because there is nothing a person does that is not psychological. This claim does not rule out the possibility that people go through a lot of emotional frustrations in the midst of all these psychologies. The first question that we should ask ourselves is: "What are these theoretical aspects

of the therapeutic dynamics of psychology?" This may lead us into the study of the various branches of psychology. For instance, when we say that 'psychology of emotion' studies how individual feelings color their experiences, it is therapeutically on the level of theory, unless a particular issue is identified and addressed.

The theoretical perspective of psychology does not take care of the immediate problem this bereaved family is going through at the moment. Yet, the therapy is that, since the awareness has been created, it is left to the concerned family members to offer the therapy or consult a counselor. In like manners, it is one thing to hold that "educational psychology" deals with the psychology of teaching and another thing, to employ it in actual fact. Until psychology has been integrated in a particular case, it remains on the level of theory. Psychology has both theoretical and practical aspects irrespective of how it guides human actions and behaviors. For example, if a person says to us: "I am having severe headache and pain here", the first therapy we can instinctively offer or employ in this particular case is: "We are sorry to hear that".

This is a perfect example of the theoretical aspect of the therapeutic dynamics of psychology. Prof. Robinson condemned the mentalist based knowledge of psychology. He advocates and advances "the proper subject of psychological investigation the actual observable behavior of human and non-human animals" (Op.cit. Robinson, Part IV. (1997:45). In the past example, it was true, we did not offer to the said sick person any physical assistance in terms of giving him some medications to relieve the pain or take him to the hospital; our response to him was therapeutic enough to get him going. Yet, our response here, though therapeutic, is purely theoretical. This compels us to reflect on the practical therapeutic nature and interactive system or dynamics of psychology – the psychological practice which digs deep into individual problems for a possible solution.

Practical Perspectives

These have got to do with more emphasis on the issues being examined in this book. Psychology ceases to be if it has no practical application to life. Having studied the meaning of psychology, its therapeutic dynamics, particularly in theory, to understand its practical dynamics becomes so essential at this point. In this aspect, we gave more examples of the various manners in which psychology had accomplished its goals in various difficult situations in which human beings had found themselves. Psychology is naturally therapeutic. It is practical when it goes extra miles to assist people in their various conditions of need – sick, loss of friendships, jobs, identity, marriage cases, broken homes, childlessness, barrenness, impotency, hatred and ill feelings, etc. According to Frick: "With man at the center" psychology, "Can take man's full range of inner experience into serious account" (Op.cit. Frick, 1987:6). In this sense, we delved into these areas of "man's full range of inner experience" within our studies on psychological practice or applied psychology.

This section raised as many questions as the following questions: "What is actually the significance of psychology in human life, especially when man's situation looks sad and miserable? Is there any human action or behavior that has no need for psychology? In which manners can somebody benefit from the practical application of psychology in his situations? Is psychology the same thing as human emotions, feelings, decisions, choices, actions, and character? Can psychology be separated from human preoccupations, professions, religions, and associations? What are the hopes and benefits the individuals and society expect to gain from psychology?" There are as many questions that can be asked as life reveals its sweet and ugly sides. It is only when our knowledge and studies on the various branches of psychology are applied and integrated into the problems that envelope our interactions and activities, that it becomes therapeutic in that instance. Openness is both therapeutic and key to healing.

However, it is sad to note that despite the therapeutic dynamics and nature of psychology, society and individuals have continued to suffer one emotional pain or the other. Is it better to summarize that "psychology: therapeutic dynamics" has remained more of a theoretical issue than practical? There are so many psychologists and experts in this cognate field out there, who no longer feel the pains and sufferings of other people. This is a devaluing of life. People should rejoice for who they are and the manner they operate and carry out their daily lives peacefully. Nobody should limit himself because of temporary setbacks. Unfortunately, many have been influenced by the elements of modernism, artificiality, and global village syndrome, selfishness and do not care to assist others in their emotional pains and situations. Therefore, this book calls individuals of all cultures to avail themselves with the therapeutic dynamics of psychology and open up themselves in love for one another.

B. PASTORAL COUNSELING FOR MINISTRY PROFESSIONALS: THE AMERICAN CASE

The use of 'American case' here alludes to an area of stress or emphasis because the subject is of universal nature. This topic is as interesting as the related texts on the area of psychological practice. I have read a lot of texts on this subject and I feel motivated to make my points on these sensitive issues that anchor on the socio-religious life of individuals and society at large, especially on my home people, Ekwerazu Umuokirika. A lot of things have been said today about pastoral care, counseling, ministries and ministry professionals as important tools in the healing of individuals and society. In a book such as this, one is compelled to raise questions as regards what constitutes pastoral care and counseling because it is from these analyses that the value of psychology vividly comes out. Or, are the two the same thing? On the other hand, when we speak of ministry professionals, who are really involved? Thereby, our ability to differentiate what ought to be and the status quo makes this section of the book more interesting. In a more practical manner, what are the techniques I need as a counselor to address the emotional concerns of others?

Eventually, from my intensive studies on psychology throughout my nursing training, down to GTF, the relevance of counseling cannot be overemphasized, especially at this present age of emotional frustrations, broken homes, marriages, joblessness, economic maladjustments and what have you. Ordinarily speaking, "Pastoral counseling for ministry professionals" seems to have been limited to those we often associate with ministries in the Church, the clergy, pastors, religious, ministers of various religious groups etc. Even at that, without the application of psychology, there will be no ministries. Thus, in this book, we shall examine the extent the ministry professionals particularly in America, have carried out their pastoral ministries amidst the various scandals encountered in different quarters today. There is no doubt that sex scandals are becoming a universal disease, occurring in various levels of human industry, in the Church, Government, offices, school systems, among the military etc. In a sense, it seems normal because of the human nature. But to observe this ugly practice in the Church, especially among those to whom the faith and therapy of so many people have been entrusted is not right or justifiably acceptable. In this light, to justify the topic at hand, we shall first of all, underline and study the terms used or employed hereupon.

Use of Terms:
In order to enlighten the minds of the uninitiated on or those who are not familiar with the issue at hand, we shall examine the following terms for the sake of clarifications as regards the enormous role of psychology in our lives:

I.   Pastoral;
II. Counseling;

III.   Ministry;

IV.   Professionals

V.   The differences between Spiritual Direction, Pastoral Care and Counseling

I.   Pastoral:

The term or adjective "pastoral" has commonly been associated with religious duties and works of evangelization, being carried out by ministers of the Christian religion, particularly pastors of the Churches and in clinical settings, among chaplains. The aim of pastoral ministry is to influence the human person to a particular way of behaving or life. For Chiew Charles the word "pastor" comes from Latin word for 'shepherd' (Charles Chiew, p. 30). Therefore, the shepherds, the pastors and pastoral care givers are the principal agents responsible for impacting religious values to their members, clients and society. Here again, one may ask if pastoral activities are limited to religious matters alone? Can pastors and pastoral care givers be charged with some social and political functions of society, even for those who do not belong to any religious organizations and those who are not their members? In other words, is pastoral work inclusive or exclusive? In Chiew's own words, *"The role of counseling within the general pastoral setting has implications for the multidimensional functions and relationships of pastors, chaplain, or member of a pastoral staff"* (Op. cit. p.40). These points will be made clearer in the course of our discussions in this book. But, let us first understand what it means to give counsel to somebody.

II.   Counseling:

The word or noun "counseling" seems to enjoy "a variety of meanings" (Op. cit. p.30). In his own words: "counsel" ...means to consult, to enter into 'confidential communion' with another person" (Op. cit. p. 33).

26

The dictionary definitions view it as an advice, a plan of action, the act of exchanging opinions and ideas, guidance, to counsel, to recommend etc." (Confer "Office Edition of the American Heritage Dictionary, 2001"). A pastoral counselor is one who officiates as spiritual advocate, who listens and gives advice on certain burning issues that affect individual lives and situations. On a larger perspective, counseling is a form of therapy, aimed at alleviating the emotional pains of the afflicted. We give advice to others not that they will accept it. People are free to listen to advices and still do what they want. According to St. Francis of Assisi: "We have been called to heal wounds, to unite what has fallen apart, and to bring home those who have lost their way" (A Guide to Religious Ministries for Catholic Men and Women, 21st Annual Edition, back of title page). This is the heart of pastoral care and counseling.

In a way, I am not just studying psychology but I want to apply it to the benefits of others. It is my candid intention to practically heal the wounds of others as Francis of Assisi noted above, unite those who have fallen apart and through professional skills, bring home those who have lost their ways by one disappointment or the other. As a nurse by profession, I have double advantages in that I encounter fellow nurses who have marriage problems, either with their husbands or children, even with friends. In legal levels, a counselor is an attorney, a trial lawyer. Counseling could be done in private, one-on-one basis or in groups with its advantages and disadvantages, as we shall see in the course of this book.

III. Ministry:

The word "ministry" is a universal application of value to service. As hinted above, "Nobody ...could actually claim that the parish is the only place for ministry to take place" (Op. cit. p. 92). It could be done in the Church, hospital or in the Government quarters. It means the act of serving others that is aimed at positive changes. The aims for this ministry may differ from individuals. For Jung in Morgan: "The path to self-knowledge, the goal of all therapy, lies in expanding the perimeters of human consciousness" (Jung in Morgan, 2010:88). The expansion is inclusive and not exclusive. There are various ministries under the sun, in the Church, Government, School systems, Military, Judiciaries, Medical and Teaching professions etc. In our context, it pertains to ministries compassionately carried out with religious undertones because I apply faith in all my scientific enquiries. It is from the nature and manner by which one carries out a particular ministry, that one may become a professional in that field.

IV. Professional:

The term "professional" comes from one's profession, that is, one's occupation that requires training, skills and specialization, and technical studies. One does not become a professional by mere identification to a particular group. For instance, in the nursing field, I am a professional because I went through the formal training and passed the board examination. One has to possess some qualities that make him or her different from others in a particular field of study to become a profession in that area. Therefore, when we speak of ministry professionals, we specifically refer to those who have the skills to effectively carry out certain tasks, ministries or services to others, be it religious, political or social, to "assist the human person cherish his own unique potential above all else in life" (Maslow in Morgan, 2010:123). There are as many professionals as there are industries, specialties, fields, institutions and organizations. Due principally to the above reasons where so many people today appear as professionals, there is need to briefly understand the differences between professionals and non-professionals in the field of pastoral and counseling activities.

V. The Differences between Spiritual Direction, Pastoral Counseling and Care:

This is an essential part of our study in this subject, psychological practice from its pastoral perspective. Practically, those who are involved with iron-related works like panel beaters, bicycle repairers, carpenters, farmers at oil fields or refineries, bricklayers, barbers etc. in many cultures, especially in my country also claim to be engineers. While we respect the principles of Marcel Gabriel who condemned the idea of evaluating people by their miniature works, professions or job they do, there is need for classes too. For instance, an assistant nurse in my Unit at the hospital cannot claim to be a registered nurse simply because he or she works in the same place with a highly skilled professional. I speak of higher professional because assistant nurses are professionals but not on equal levels with doctors or registered nurses. This is where it is important to understand what makes a pastoral care giver different from a pastoral counselor and a spiritual director. A pastoral or spiritual caregiver can be a pastoral counselor only when he has acquired the skills and knowledge for both fields and ministries. We have already and clearly noted that ministry extends beyond the church confines, services to other related areas of human need, be it in the hospital, government, military, industry, school etc.

Therefore, the words 'ministry and pastor' enjoy a wide panorama of meanings. A clergyman cannot claim to be a pastor or minister in all respects. There are limits a priest, pastor, and minister, can claim or go in these areas of psychological practice that involve competences, skills and professionalism. A clergyman is primarily trained to bring the good news of the kingdom to people. But because of the sophisticated society we live in, many clergymen have undertaken to pursue different fields of study in order to be properly equipped for their ministries. Some are professional counselors, care givers and spiritual directors. It is professional too to examine these fields of study more closely. These distinctions are necessary so that when a pastoral or spiritual caregiver is faced with human crisis that demands a professional, the solution can easily be sought from the appropriate skills. This process equally demands humility on the part of those who may claim to be jack-of-all-trades but masters of none. Hence, we shall present and treat these related-disciplines in this order:

a.   Spiritual Direction:

In ordinary man's knowledge of the word, spirituality pertains to God and heaven. In this light therefore, any person who is engaged in spiritual exercises like praying, going to Church, reading the bible, is either undergoing some spiritual direction or called upon to prepare people to be at peace with God and for going to heaven. This is where the clergy come in as spiritual directors. Even in spiritual direction, psychology is employed. Yet among the priests, some of them are appointed to serve in this capacity as professionals. In a layman's knowledge, every priest is called upon to give spiritual direction to those he is shepherding. A priest, minister or pastor cannot, because he gives spiritual direction to his congregation, begins to officiate as pastoral counselor or pastoral care giver in all respects. However, both pastoral care, counseling and spiritual direction seem to be swimming in the same pool, interwoven but at times, in different directions and that is what makes this study very interesting. Thus, we are constrained to examine what spiritual direction means generally and specifically in our own context here. Does one become a spiritual director because one is a clergyman, pastor or minister in the church?

Actually, spiritual direction is not limited to the confines of the clergy or ministers of the Gospel message. According to Liz Budd Ellmann:

Spiritual direction is the process of accompanying people on a spiritual journey. Spiritual direction exists in a context that emphasizes growing closer to God (or the sacred, the holy or a higher power). It explores a deeper relationship with spiritual aspect of being human (Liz Budd Ellmann, Internet website).

In another development, James Keegan remarked: "Spiritual direction is the contemplative practice of helping another person or group to awaken to the mystery called God in all of life and to respond to that discovery in a growing relationship of freedom and commitment" (James Keegan, Internet website).

Spiritual direction, according to Wikipedia is:

The practice of being with people as they attempt to deepen their relationship with the divine, or to learn and grow in their own personal spirituality. The person seeking direction shares stories of his or her encounters of the divine, or how he or she is experiencing spiritual issues. The director listens and asks questions to assist the directee in his or her process of reflection and spiritual growth (Wikipedia, the free Encyclopedia).

The emphasis in all these expressions is on "spiritual growth". By implication, it is obvious that spiritual direction is not counseling or pastoral counseling as such. While the emphasis on spiritual direction is based on the longing for spiritual advancement, counseling is centered on immediate solutions that may not have anything to do with going to heaven. That is why in the Catholic Church, spiritual direction addresses matters of faith, the saints, angels, demons, heaven, hell, purgatory and other spiritual issues. The subject matter of both spiritual direction and pastoral counseling is man and his problems, but the approach to these problems depends on its nature. Every human case or problem has to be treated differently and singly as a unique one. For instance, you cannot apply the same skills or approach the case of Mr. 'A' who lost his wife the same way you would on Mr. 'B' who equally lost his wife. Yes, both lost their wives. But Mr. 'B' may have family members who console and support him while Mr. 'A' has none.

That is why in the understanding of Nwachukwu, a spiritual caregiver or spiritual director may not be 'religious' because, according to him, "Spirituality is holistic" (Nwachukwu. 2010:163), incorporating the minutes details of human activity and behaviors. In this sense, a spiritual director should, in a practical manner, be all things to all men, a pastoral counselor, pastoral care giver, a religious, a teacher etc., and one who offers the best professional and non-professional assistance to others for their personal enhancement and progress. On a different note, I still know some of my friends who were advised to seek spiritual directions for the problems they face in their homes as noted already. In this capacity, there is no problem offering spiritual direction to troubled families, but the emphasis is how the said direction is being given. For instance, I have seen cases where some clergymen would simply dismiss disturbing issues in the family with the wave of the hand.

In more direct manner, I still remember the story my mother told me regarding his sister who had little problem with her husband. These are staunch Catholics. As it were, when that my aunt approached her parish priest and told him that her husband was returning late every night, the priest told her it was a common problem with many men and that she should pray over it and stop worrying herself. In essence, the priest did not listen to my aunt's pains and understand what she was going through. My studies today have revealed that the priest was not a professional in terms of pastoral counseling. The fault was not his but on the lack of skills to handle such unique cases. But, he felt he had given the best spiritual direction to my aunt. Pastoral counseling is a two-way or more than three-way process where the counselor and counselee establish an environment where their meetings and discussions would be cordial and friendly. In the above story, the priest did not make any efforts to assist her solve her misunderstanding with the husband. Thus, my aunt left the priest more disappointed than she was with her husband.

In both spiritual direction and pastoral counseling, patience and time are needed. A professional spiritual director studies the situation before jumping to a solution. The uninformed priest in our story was not to blame because he did not know the procedures to follow in such intricate matters that involved some techniques. Spiritual direction and pastoral counseling are far beyond the celebration of the sacraments or preaching the Gospel message. While every clergyman should give spiritual directions to his parishioners, it is important to learn more about human psychological problems and the best manners to approach or address them. The next topic we would like to examine at this point is pastoral care. We have seen that popularly speaking, spiritual caregiver is the same person as pastoral caregiver. But a pastoral care giver may not be a spiritual director or a pastoral counselor. Then, what is precisely "pastoral care?"

b.   Pastoral Care:

This can be understood as an aspect and within the context of pastoral counseling. Pastoral care specifically points to the various steps taken to access the needs of others in the face of problems and the ability to respond empathetically to them. This purely demands a psychological process. These problems could be sickness, loss of beloved ones, loneliness due to lack of friendships, family members, lack of jobs, prayers to be offered to the dead members of some families etc. Pastoral care is most often relative because the one that is carried out in a hospital setting does not share sameness with the ones carried out in individual homes or military. The content may be same, related to the care of souls, but the method of emphasis differs from one to the other. That is why pastoral care has its own theology and psychology. For instance, according to Internet resources:

> *Pastoral care or spiritual care is a ministry to any person who is experiencing a period of personal, social, physical, material, mental, spiritual or moral stress. Pastoral care reaches out to such people wherever they are suffering, offering consolation and support in whatever form is appropriate to the person at the time (Wikipedia, free Internet encyclopedia).*

Pastoral counseling does give assistance to people in various situations but with a different perspective, approach and techniques. This is why pastoral counseling is different from pastoral or spiritual care and direction. Pastoral care is a professional process whereby pastoral care givers offer assistance to those who have emotional and psychological frustrations due to sickness, death of a family member, pitiable situation as such.

Pastoral care goes beyond the confines of the church and religious organizations as we indicated before. A non-professional can equally give care to others. It is part of nature that we assist one another in times of sickness, bereavements and other needs. We can also refer to this act as 'pastoral' because it is "a literary or other artistic work that portrays or evokes rural life, usually in an idealized manner" (Office Edition of the American Heritage Dictionary, 2001). This is not comparable with pastoral care in the strict sense of it. In this book, we are discussing pastoral care on its professional level. This discussion will best be appreciated after we shall have studied and examined the meaning of "pastoral counseling".

c. Pastoral counseling

In the words of the American Association of Pastoral Counselors, "Pastoral counseling is a unique form of counseling which uses spiritual resources as well as psychological understanding for healing and growth... (Wikipedia, the free Encyclopedia). In every act of pastoral counseling, psychological tools are necessarily employed. The major instrument for this process is attentive listening skill. Pastoral counseling is a branch of counseling in which psychologically trained ministers, rabbis, priests and other persons provide therapeutic services. It is true that in pastoral care, spiritual direction and care, therapy is envisaged, but here emphasis is mainly placed on ontological and supernatural dimensions or interventions. While pastoral counseling may equally employ spiritual values in its process, the main resources are derived from psychological values and techniques. A pastoral counselor equally employs understanding and expression of the pastoral relationship. In this instance, "Pastoral counseling uses both psychologically and theological resources to deepen its understanding of the pastoral relationship" (Ibid).

Here come the differences. Pastoral and spiritual care providers are always affiliated to one faith or religious tradition. On the contrary, a person who has no religion can effectively offer pastoral counseling to clients provided he or she is trained in the management systems. While some clients, who have no religion of their own, are free to accept or reject pastoral or spiritual care, the pastoral and spiritual care providers do limit their ministries to the members of their religious traditions or denominations. But a well-trained pastoral counselor cuts across religious barriers and differences and offer therapy to clients of any group or religion. No wonder, according to Internet sources:

Some pastoral counselors have developed special training programs to encourage cooperation between religious

*professionals and medical professionals on treatment of
issues like addiction, since spirituality is an important part of
recovery for many people (Ibid).*

The above assertion seems to have led to the debate among some
quarters whether pastoral counseling is the same as other forms
of counseling and psychotherapy. As stated already, while pastoral
counseling does not claim to substitute other forms of counseling,
it shares some resemblances and relationships with them. Besides,
while pastoral or spiritual care can be offered to the mentally retarded
and the unconscious or to the dead, "Pastoral counseling can only be
offered to the conscious and to people who are aware of their problem
and are capable of making a decision and changing after providing
the necessary insight" (Benner, 2003:20-21). As for the context of
pastoral or spiritual care, it can take place in hospitals, nursing homes,
rehabilitation facilities, independent living centers, psychiatric
facilities, correctional institutions, and residential care facilities etc.

But on the other hand, according to Benner, especially regarding its
setting, "Pastoral counseling, like any other form of counseling, is
structured. It is a practice that is marked by formality and not a practice
that should be done anyhow and anywhere" (Ibid). Besides, while
pastoral spiritual care may not require an appointment or a venue,
pastoral counseling must have all these – appointments and venues.
In this capacity, in involving all forms of counseling, Benner identified
three stages. These stages have their corresponding tasks in pastoral
counseling and they are: encounter, engagement, and disengagement
stages. We shall examine them in their order of arrangement, thus:

1. Encounter Stage:

This is the preliminary stage in every pastoral counseling session.
It is initial meeting of the pastoral counselor and the counselee or

the one seeking help. The Counselor's goal or focus at this instance is to make sure he establishes a dimensional or personal contact with the client. This stage is so important because, the counselor has to set the boundaries for the counseling relationship, and get "acquainted with the client and his or her central concerns, conduct a pastoral diagnosis, and develop a mutually acceptable focus for the work they will do together" (Benner 2003:72). According to Goldboorm: "Getting to know the client as a person...his or her age, social and economic background, racial or cultural background, marital status, and the problem that brought him or her to counseling" (Goldboom, 2006:2-3), is of fundamental importance in any counseling session. This stage is very essential for the success of the counseling session because it is here that the counselor "allays the fears and concerns of the client" (Corey & Corey, 2006:36). In the view of Benner: "It is from this stage, that the pastor [counselor], in addition to his or her personal dispositions, begins to put into practice the counseling skills" (Op.Cit. 2003:75), especially his listening skill. This process of relationship building through listening, Miller et al refers to it as "the clarification stage" (Miller et al, 1995:16).

2. Engagement Stage:

This is the liminal or working stage where the counselor builds the heart of the counseling relationship. This is the "business" stage because both the counselor and the client have to get down to the issue or splinters that brought them together or necessitated the counseling session or client into counseling, and this may occupy one to three sessions. In Benner's view, the task of the pastoral counselor in this stage is to "explore the client's feelings, thoughts, and behavioral patterns that are associated with the problem area, as well as the development of new perspectives and strategies for coping or change (Op.Cit., 2003:74).

3. Disengagement Stage:

As the caption suggests, at this stage, the counseling session has come to a close. It is also known as "termination or final stage in other forms of counseling" (Op.Cit., 2006:3). It does not just bring the session to an end but it also involves "an evaluation of progress and an assessment of remaining concerns, a referral for further help if need be, and the termination of the counseling relationship" (Benner, 2003:74). Termination in this case involves three things:

(a) Recapitulation or the counselor looking back and reviewing with clients what they have learned, changes made if possible and how they have changed or progressed;

(b) Looking forward, in which the counselor and client set an ending date, discuss future plans, and consider the need for additional counseling sessions or referral;

(c) Here, both the counselor and counselee say goodbye to each other. That is, in this instance, the client expresses thanks to the counselor and both share their feelings about ending and saying their farewell (Hill, 2004:410).

C. THE DILEMMA OF PASTORAL COUNSELING FOR MINISTRY PROFESSIONALS

The choice and dedication of one's life to the service of God and humanity are much different from choosing a career. In the choice of a career or an occupation, it may involve personal determinations, choice levels, job characteristics, desired income levels, and place or location preferences etc. In career choice, personal interests come first. Unlike in the case of what one aims to be in life, regardless of profits or gains, this involves a decision also to live primarily for the benefits of others. In religious perspective, it is regarded as vocation, a calling to serve society in selfless capacities. People in this second option go with the maxim: "We are created in God's own image, and we must aspire to be with him in service to society and neighbors".

It is within this category that we see the clergy; religious, men and women dedicate themselves for the service of God and humanity. Yet, the greatest question and concern that face this book is to ascertain whether those who claim to have dedicated themselves to God and to the service of others are realistic to their calling. As Connor would have it: "When one makes an external manifestation the essence of a religious career, this essence is simply too shallow to subsist" (Fr. Stephen J. Connor, C.S.P, 2000: A-4). On the contrast, a call to service draws us out of ourselves by the interest we have in others and the public. In his own words: "The public life gives us the chance to lose ourselves in others and thereby find ourselves healed and whole and again" (Parker J. Palmer, cited in Dieter T. Hessel, 1992:124). Losing ourselves in others entails the application of psychological practice, because, according to Capuzzi & Gross, as cited in Nwachukwu, "The manner in which people think and feel affect their lives" (Capuzzi & Gross, 2003:214 in Nwachukwu, 2011:8). It is sheer psychotic losing oneself in a person that is unreliable. In a sense, the dilemma involved in this section or discussion extends to the following:

a. Aim of Pastoral Counseling or Care:

Many Christians and their pastors tend to perceive this function as limited to the members of the same Christian group. Just as Hessel would put it, "When one refers to 'pastoral ministry' today, the prevailing image is that of pastors shepherding persons who are already in the fold, by means of clinical counseling" (Hessel, p. 124). This should not be the focal point of pastoral ministry and counseling. The primary role of professional Church workers is to equip the faith community to intervene compassionately in social systems that are not limited to any group of people.

Having taken note that the primary aim of pastoral care and counseling is to assist people in various emotional and social problems, ministry professionals equally include lay people who are cultured in the skills to respond to people's spiritual needs also. To develop the congregation's capability to do more effective pastoral care requires a working knowledge of personal, family, group, and community dynamics. Eventually, by this dynamics, the knowledge of psychology has to be applied. Thus, we continue to ask that fundamental question: "Is there anything any human being does under the sun that is not psychological in nature?" Here lie the values of psychology in life and its healing capacity.

There are so many social problems individuals go through in their lives, inhuman housing, shortage of medical attention, homelessness, abject poverty, sexist oppressions, economic victimizations, etc. At times, others may not perceive that there are people in these conditions, hence the need for this book. These problems are the subject of pastoral care and counseling. Therefore, the scope and horizons of ministry professionals should be widened today to include all these too. Days are gone when ministry professionals are limited to the clergy and pastors of souls. The lay apostolate has major role to play to bring healing to people in various difficulties. Even in Church services, the pastors alone cannot be expected to do the reading, preach, sing, and give Holy Communion (in case of the Catholic Church) etc. Ministry has grown into a fellowship in which each person has a role to play as a professional and this practice makes group counseling or therapy fascinating. In keeping with Sullivan's overall worldview, "...It is imperative that the therapist (or counselor) understands that his role is primarily that of a 'participant observer', for, despite all protestations to the contrary from traditionalists, the therapist becomes necessarily part of an interpersonal, face-to-face relationship with the patient" (Sullivan in Morgan, 2010:192).

b. Biblical orientations:

There are many instances in the bible to prove the unlimited nature of pastoral care and counseling. The emphasis is on the individual at the moment who needs assistance here and now and not on faith traditions or members. In the Gospel of John, we read:

> *I am the door; if any one enters by me, he [or she] will be saved, and will go in and out and find pasture....I am the good shepherd; I know my own and my own know me.... I have other sheep that are not of this fold; I must bring them also, and they will heed my voice. So there shall be one flock, one shepherd. (John 10: 9-16).*

The shepherd has a universal intent, consistent with the purpose of the preexisting Word, a unifying one and not two. The same hint was repeated in Ezekiel, where the ministry of "the shepherd extends to caring of the sick, the weak, crippled, strayed, and lost and keeps them from becoming food for all the wild beasts" (Ezekiel, 34: 1-16). The ethical intention is "to feed them in justice... and to make with them a "covenant of peace" (Ezekiel, 34: 16, 25).

c. The 'woes' of pastoral counseling and care in our time:

We do not intend to dwell much on this subject. Listen to the Radios, watch the TVs, read the News Papers, and discover the scandals created by some of the so-called ministry professionals especially here in America. The scandal is gradually becoming a worldwide issue that corrodes the foundation of the Pastoral counseling and care. In my culture, the Igbo of Nigeria, we describe the situation as "nkita tara okpukpu anyawara ya n'olu". That literally means: "The dog that has eaten the bone hung on its neck", which it was meant to protect. Some ministry professionals have betrayed the pastoral responsibilities placed on their shoulders by leading innocent boys and girls who were entrusted to their care, into the worse behaviors that will affect their faith and lives forever – the pedophilic cases. This is a serious problem plaguing the Church, the principal ministry professional and her ministers in our time. A stop must be put to it.

Consequently, there should be an urgent call to reformation and orientation among pastoral counselors and ministry professionals. To recapitulate our stand on this issue, pastoral care and counseling should be extended to everyone who needs it, not within the clinical setting alone. The time has come when the lay people should fully be incorporated as part and parcel of ministry professionals by assigning them some functions in pastoral care and counseling through some in-service training on the relevant programs, skills and strategies. Private counseling is as important as group counseling and the latter has to be emphasized the more. We are in the age where people go through a lot of social, religious, political, emotional and economic problems. Pastoral counseling and care have to be critically re-examined the more as most of the ministry professionals capitalize on them for their own selfish ends.

At this juncture, I am compelled to examine specific works of some experts or professionals as already noted in this work, to buttress the value of psychology in general. Some experts have tried to study human interactions and came out with important strategies and guidelines that serve as springboards for authentic existence. In this section, I shall study the life stories of these experts because the pattern of life an individual lives colors the ways he or she sees the world. These life experiences are the foundations for psychology. Thus, I have decided to examine the works of few psychotherapists and what influenced them to arrive at the unique position of the knowledge of psychology they hold today in the field of psychological practice in general. These studies will actually throw light to some of the emotional problems many go through in their lives today. Some of these problems can easily be understood and solved if the appropriate approaches are made by experts. These professionals include: Carl Ransom Rogers,

D. CARL RANSOM ROGERS AND PERSON-CENTERED PSYCHOTHERAPY

Experts like Carl Rogers have highlighted the need for psychological practice from a person-centered approach. This is the apogee of our enquiry, in which the need of the individual agent is involved and considered dimensionally. In a way, from Roger's person-centered psychotherapy, this book is boosted both in content and scope. Therefore, we are going to study the need of this aspect of applied psychology from three substantial histories of Roger's life. We shall do so in this order, after few observations:

1. His life story and part of his achievement;

2. His key theories;

3. Integration and application of his life and works in everyday occurrence.

I have heard so much about Carl Rogers, especially during one of my studies in psychology. But I have not actually studied his life stories, works, theories and achievements as close as I have done recently. However, there are a lot of things that can be said about his life, theories and implications and of his philosophy or beliefs for the present day society and even for the Church, which are intentionally omitted in this book. To include every detail about this great Psychotherapist, we need to write another book. Unfortunately, as noted, because of the limited nature of this enquiry or writing, I am going to select those I consider essential. For instance, I read three textbooks on this very subject or man, namely: "Beginning with Freud" of Morgan, "On becoming Carl Rodgers" of Kirschenbaum, and "On becoming a Person" by Rogers himself. All of them point to the same and one person.

There is no gainsaying that Rogers is the grandfather of modern pastoral psychology and the father of person-centered psychotherapy, based on the implication of his writings. I have the belief that by the time any person finishes reading Carl Rogers, he will, in one way or the other, become part of Rogers. Nothing could be beneficial or important to anybody than being respected for who he is. Respect itself is therapeutic too. The human person is and remains the starting point of psychology and whatever else anybody has to say about him, respecting his values is paramount. There may be doubt that psychology extends to the manners human beings relate to animals, (which sounds illogical from scientific point of view), yet humans are still the starting point of such inquiries or scientific investigations. In this way, the works of Rogers remain a big challenge for other psychologists who tend to emphasize ritualistic approach to psychology – 'it has to be this way all the time' attitude. At this point, one may ask: "Who is Carl Rogers?"

I. Life story and part of his achievements:

Boyhood life:

The boyhood experience of Carl Rogers was more of a mixed one. He followed his parents' directives without questioning them. In the present day standards, Rogers belonged to the upper-middle class and educated family. The achievements of his grandfather, Alexander Hamilton Rogers and those of his parents were big incentives for him to face life with greater optimism. Being the fourth child of other six siblings, born on January 8, 1902, proved he came from a very large family in Oak Park in Illinois. In Morgan's words, "His father, Walter Alexander Rogers, was a civil engineer and his mother, Julia Crushing Rogers, devout Christian woman and traditional housewife" (Morgan, H. John. p. 155).

The engineering work of his father kept him away from the family most of the time and because of that, Rogers was so attached to his mother, to the point that he initially seemed to become a fundamentalist with Christianity like his mother.

As a young brilliant boy, he started to read at the age of four, attempted and read the Bible from Genesis to Revelation.

Eventually, at the age of six, he attended Holmes School, and being very smart for first-grader reader, was moved to second-grader reader, down to the forth. Even one of his second grader classmates, Helen Elliott, who later became his wife, recalled his brilliance. He had the ability to read 300 pages in three hours at this early stage. He always strove to take the first position in any human achievement. Rogers seemed to be addicted to reading that he read even encyclopedias and dictionaries. His parents, though, with college education, could not understand the young boy's ambition in reading, fantasies, storytelling, and adventure stories etc. His mother's frequent joke as reported by Kirschenbaum was: "There you are again with your nose in a book" (Kirschenbaum, Howard. p. 4). His father took him to so many places, various construction sites, South and East, Chicago, New Orleans, Norfolk, Virginia even to Britain. He later traveled on his own to the Orient, Hawaii, Japan, Korea, China, Hong Kong and the Philippines, Germany, France, England. His experiences, particularly at the Philippines regarding poor children and prisoners equally affected his view of life. Besides, he kept journal of his activities and voyages/trips for educational purposes.

II. Family Prayer Life:

There were many sayings of Rogers that singled him out as a devoted psychologist. Permit me to quote his utterances in Kirschenbaum's commentary:

> *They were both devoted and loving parents, giving a great deal of time and energy to creating a family life, which would 'hold' the children in the way in which they should go. ...I do not remember ever being given a direct command on an important subject, yet such was the unity of our family that it was understood by all that...'Other persons behave in dubious ways which we do not approve of in our family. Many of them play cards, go to movies, smoke, dance, drink, and engage in other activities, some unmentionable"* (*Op. Cit. p. 6, Morgan, p.156).*

This prayerful life guided him in keeping honest records of the sales of his mother's farm produce. The grace of God works effectively and only when one is honest and kind. The very statement, "I do not remember ever being given a direct command on an important subject" guided his philosophy of life, as we shall see later. He embraced Christianity as long as it brought people working together for a common goal and as one family and not necessarily for achieving eternal rewards. But his trip to the Orient had drastic effect on him. According to Kirschenbaum:

> *He came to believe that good works were more important than ritual or doctrine in Christianity. One must take responsibility of one's actions.... Thus, his views on many religious, political,*

social and economic questions changed considerably as a result...(Kirschenbaum, p. 29).

He became more self-confident, curious and conscious in his ability to move forward in life. Becoming more empirical oriented, he desired to investigate the truth of his received belief systems from his family background.

III. Higher Education:

Because most members of his family have studied at the University of Wisconsin, he felt comfortable to study there too. Having being cultured in family agriculture, he aimed to graduate in scientific agriculture. This was a turning point in his life because he has to leave parental guidance and define his own life goals and aspirations. However, his religious influences played much role in his college education. For instance, he joined the 'Ag – Triangle,' being a group of agricultural students meeting under the auspices of the Y.M.C.A., under the leadership of Professor George Humphrey" (Op. Cit. p. 19).

With his new acquaintances and new horizons at various conventions, especially "The Des Moines" different from the cloistered life of the family, Rogers started to stick to a life aspiration of his own, not influenced by anybody. Yet, this very convention was the climax of his faith in God to a point that he wrote: "I have found what I never found before, the peace of God which pass-eth all understanding" (Op. Cit. p. 21). Chosen at his third year at the University to be one of the United States Youth Delegates to the W.S.C.F.C. in Peking; China in April 1922, tremendous changes came to his life. Hard work goes a long way to bring healing in one's life.

The aim of the conference was to learn more about how to evangelize the world and win souls for God in their time. He provided what he regarded as "China Diary" for keeping records of what transpired there. But for him: "I consider this a time when I achieved my psychological independence" (Morgan, p. 157). By that, he meant that he had won his own freedom from parental 'dictatorship' as it were, and can now think freely as a person. That is precisely what psychological practice aims at, equipping people to enjoy the best of their lives without much pressure from outsiders. Dictatorship here is understood in the context of liberation from received ideologies, theologies and doctrines. He did not just accept the person of Jesus, he wanted to know the truth and who he was and how such knowledge could impact his behaviors in future. In his own words: "One way of putting this is that I feel I have become more adequate in letting myself be what I am" (Rogers, R. Carl. P. 17).

As luck would have it, he returned back to the University of Wisconsin and earned his B.A in history in 1924, after the World Christian Federation's Conference in Peking. This was also the very year he got married to his second grader classmate, Helen Elliot after so many years of dating and deliberations. His marriage life was a welcome event as he got settled with his own soul mate, a marriage that was blessed with two children – a boy and a girl. With his burning interest in the world of psychology, he and his wife moved to New York, where he pursued the dream of his life at Union Theological Seminary, while at the same time, bagging a master's degree from Columbia University. Having worked at the Institute of Child Guidance for some years, developed keen interest for psychotherapy from where he got masters in psychology in 1928 and doctorate in psychotherapy in 1931. As it were, Rogers spent substantial period of his time at Rochester Society for developing personal operational theories and therapy techniques. He worked for the delinquent and underprivileged children as his experiences in the Philippines were still afresh in his mind.

Eventually, he received a full professorial appointment at the Ohio State University, an offer he did not accept initially till his wife encouraged him to do so. As a professor, having taught for some time, from 1940–1945, published his first book entitled: "*Counseling and Psychotherapy: Newer Concepts in Practice*" (Morgan, p. 159). This great publication seems to have become the foundation of modern psychotherapy today and the synthesis of psychological practice. Shortly after he had published his masterpiece, he was appointed in New York as Director of counseling Services for the United Service Organization in 1944. Besides this, he was offered a post at the Counseling Center of the University of Chicago where he served from 1945 – 1957. Of course in 1951, he wrote his most famous book: *Client-Centered Therapy: Its Current Practice, Implications, and Theory*" (Ibid).

At the end of 1957, he took up a "joint post at the University of Wisconsin as both Professor of Psychology and Professor of psychiatry" (Op. Cit. p.160).

He joined so many other Western Behavioral Sciences, gave the 1947 Presidential address at the American Psychological Association, developed his "*On Becoming a Person*", that was published 1961. Not only that he was honored world over for his psychological input, he was also nominated for the 'Noble Peace prize' in his work with national inter-group conflict in South Africa and Northern Ireland" (Op. Cit. p. 161).

Despites all the honorary degrees he received from so many Universities, as early as 1944, he was the President of the American Psychological Association. In 1956, he became the first president of the American Academy of Psychotherapists and in 1964 was selected as the Humanist of the year by the American Humanist Association... and in 1972; the American Psychological Association awarded him the coveted Distinguished Professional Award" (Ibid). Consequently, most of these writings and publications or texts became classic and fundamental in theory and practice for modern psychology and psychotherapy. Hence, my choice of reviewing his books here.

IV. His key theories:

From our studies and examinations of the writings of Carl R. Rogers, we shall consider the following theories that have assisted me in developing the course of psychological practice in this book:

a. Theory of Personality Development;

b. Client-centered theory of personality and psychotherapeutic treatment

c. Humanist theory;

d. Phenomenological perspective;

- Self-actualizing tendency;
- Subjective versus objective reality of psychotherapy;
- The 'self-concept' theory;
- Unconditional Positive regard;
- Freudian notion of personality and that of Rogers;
- Incongruity/Religion

There are so many things Carl Rogers believed in and taught others as well. Some of these aspects of knowledge appear new in the field of psychological practice. Some even tend to contradict our basic beliefs in psychologists like Sigmund Freud's concept of personality development. We shall briefly present each of these concepts and theories as we enlisted them above:

a. *Theory of personality development:*

For Rogers, each person has the inclination or tendency to become the best individual he naturally is meant to be. Commenting on this, Morgan noted: "Rogers firmly believed that at the core, every human being is fundamentally good, being essentially purposive, forward-moving, constructive, realistic, and trustworthy" (Op. Cit. p. 165). It is self-rewarding that psychology recognizes the basic and unique nature of the human person at the moment. For Rogers, nobody is completely a fool. Thanks to Rogers, the need to capture one's self esteem and meaning in life is basic and encouraging.

b. *Client-centered theory of personality and psychotherapeutic treatment*

Therefore, in the theory, client's needs and concerns come first before the counselor. This is where the 3 major elements that characterize his theory of personality come in, namely; the counselor has to:

(1) Create an atmosphere where the client can trust him or her as we noted during our discussion on the 3 stages of pastoral counseling; (2) Present him or herself as one trying to enter the client's own world of feeling, and finally; (3) Create enough ground for mutual trust to be established for their meeting (Consult, Morgan p. 164). In Morgan's words: "First, two persons are in psychological contact such that each of them is fully aware that the other's presence makes a difference" (Op. Cit. p. 164).

In effect, this book is geared towards assisting counselors and skilled individuals enter into other's own world of feeling. It is basically through this professional way that most of the issues people have which are beyond the ice-berg or surface diagnosis can be understood and healed.

c. *Humanist theory*

In line with his theory of personality development, a psychologist or psychotherapist has to be human, one who does not assume superiority over the client. As Kirschenbaum noted of Rogers, "I am inclined to believe that fully to be a human being is to enter into the complex process of being one of the most widely sensitive, responsive, creative, and adaptive creatures on this planet" (Kirschenbaum, p. 250). To confirm the above assertion, Rogers insists that: "I believe it will be clear that a person who is involved in the directional process which I have termed 'the good life' is creative person" (Rogers, p. 193). In this way, a person is sensible enough to stand on his initiatives, make decisions and act on them without external forces or intending to create stress for others. Practically, Rogers has reminded each person that he or she has the ability to set course of his or her own life. We cannot delay or postpone what can be achieved today because of lack of self-confidence. Each person has that audacity and capability to assert himself and live.

In this light, he is an existential psychologist and philosopher. Like Gabriel Marcel in *his phenomenological* understanding, Rogers holds that each person is intrinsically good and deserves the best for who he holistically is and not to be judged on one aspect of his life. This conviction led him to speak of the following:

a. *"Actualizing tendency"*. It refers to the innate or "deriving force in human nature towards the good and self-fulfillment" (Morgan, p. 166).

b. *"Subjective versus objective reality of psychotherapy"*. In every form of psychotherapy, the subjective aspect as noted earlier should not be allowed to conflict with the counselor's role. Maximum regard and consideration has to be given to either side.

c. *"Self-concept" in Rogers.* This refers to how the person perceives himself authentically without interferences. Any situation or scenario that creates a different picture, other than what the person really is or feels, creates a threat. [Consult, Morgan, p.p. 171 – 173].

d. *"Unconditional positive regard"* For Rogers, in Morgan: "This requires every individual to be accepted and respected for who and what they are, without conditions of ifs, ands, or buts" (Op. Cit. p. 171).

e. *Freudian notion of personality development and that of Rogers.* They all agree that man is progressive and purposeful. The difference is the structure of Freud's personality, especially on the fact that the "id" is characterized by selfishness and greed. Rogers opposes that because of the natural disposition of man for good.

f. *Incongruity and religion.* We emphasize all these to bring out the theories of Rogers. He calls this a "basic estrangement in man" (Op. Cit. p. 170). As each person has the natural tendency to be good, any obstruction to achieving this aim creates incongruence or disagreement. This equally happens in religion, where people are forced to behave in certain manners to please or avoid offending God or neighbor. For Rogers, it is not healthy for a person who has no intention for evil. It is always better for one to be oneself in whatever one is doing.

V. Application and integration of the works of Rogers to life

The first thing I have to say here is that Rogers has influenced my choice of topic in this book or project. His understanding of psychology and psychotherapy is clear and easily comprehensible. From his writings, I have deduced the following values:

His boyhood and school age:

- ❖ Need to listen to one's parents especially when one is at their care;

- ❖ Industrious parental background is important in the forming of a child;

- ❖ Once God is at the foundation of the family, blessings flourish there;

- ❖ Importance of prayer is highlighted in the family and success of Rogers;

- ❖ Hard work and discipline are always beneficial and therapeutic;

- ❖ Procrastination is idleness and dangerous;

- ❖ Good education is the primary key to success;

- ❖ Good parents, companions and friendships are treasures and gifts;

- ❖ Marriage with one's own choice or heart is also a blessing.

The family is the foundation for nurturing a child, good life, society. Because Rogers enjoyed an ideal family background, he felt life was that way. The need to appreciate one's family and environments is basic and enlightening. Nothing can be more rewarding in one's life except having an environment where peace abounds.

His Theories:

- ❖ Need to respect the dignity of the human person;

- ❖ "No person is completely useless" (Nwachukwu, O. Anthony, p. xxviii), even the criminal in a prison/custody;

- ❖ Regard people and treat them for who they are and not by the judgments we set for them. This is a big lesson to me in my nursing profession;

- ❖ Love others whether they love back or not, for that is the ideal thing to do;

- ❖ Religion should not be practiced to avoid punishment by the Church/God. It should be born out of one's own conviction and faith;

- ❖ Ritualism and doctrines are not the basis for faith, but good work;

- ❖ Individual potentials should be put in full use and not be allowed to rot away; for each person as such is accountable for his success in life;

- ❖ Self-confidence and reliance are the major keys to science/success.

Rogers has really given us food for thought and the principles of being good people. But, I disagree with him on his later attitude to religion. How can he turn to bite the finger that fed him? He claimed to have seen Jesus in religion in his early boyhood. Education should not conflict with one's basic faith in the Supernatural. After all, Rogers could not deny that those positive values of religion he imbibed in his family did not assist him to accomplish his desired goals or educational aspirations. While I do agree with Rogers that man is purposeful and positive oriented, it is not true that he has no inclination to sin or do something bad. In the first place, this is against the basic teaching of the Catholic faith on 'Original sin'. However, Rogers was speaking from the point of view of sticking on doing the right thing irrespective of the sins of Adam and Eve, maintaining that every person is accountable for his or her sins and actions and nobody else.

As Catholic, I believe that the sin of our first parents has effects on us today. While there are good people in the world, bad people seem to outweigh the good ones. Then, if it is true that corruption, inhumanity to man exists in society and we know and experience it on daily basis, why would Rogers make us believe in such an ideal world where every man is a saint. Such teaching is obnoxious. On the other side, Rogers seems to have advocated for a lawless society where the concept of law is not expedient. He advocates for a society where people should always act creditably, do things right and fully enjoy the fruits of happy lives.

However, based on his primary concern for the human person, I give him 100%. Life can be better than it is today if people were to act true to their nature in good works. Even if man is both positive and negative, the possibility of choosing the positive aspect is always there, if people can stick to truth and justice. Therefore, I am invigorated to join Rogers in his pastoral psychotherapy and work for the betterment of the human condition, by respecting and accepting others as they really are without my subjective judgments. Consequently, this is the aim, value of psychological practice and its pastoral implications on individuals and society, as we shall see in the life of another Psychotherapist, Harry Sullivan, are enormous. Good life style is virtuous and creates and recreates life itself.

E. HARRY STACK SULLIVAN AND INTERPERSONAL PSYCHOANALYSIS

In view of the target of this book, psychological practice in the hidden lives of people demand an urgent attention, especially today that a lot of people face emotional problems. Basing our study on the works of Sullivan from the point of view of their psychological implication and value to society, we shall study and concentrate more on his interpersonal psychoanalysis and examine the impacts such fields of study have made on the progress, success and total integration of the human person. We shall approach this study from the following outline:

A. It's introduction

B. Brief and informed summary of his life, education, and professional practice

C. Key Theories that made him famous

D. Analysis of his work and its relevance in today's society

A. Brief Introduction:

After reading and reflecting on Harry Stack Sullivan's work on interpersonal psychoanalysis, I was convinced without any doubt in my mind as a Nurse that he was really and practically the father of modern social psychiatry. Today, many people claim to be psychologists, psychiatrist doctors, psychoanalysts based solely on their knowledge and practice of medicine. Reading through Sullivan's work, reminds me of the interpersonal relationships that should exist between doctors, nurses and the patients. These are the values psychology holds for humanity. Most often, many medical professionals care less of this aspect of human nature, which should be fundamental to the whole healing process from inside out. Some emphasize more on their paychecks than the lives of those they take care of. In this way, psychology calls them to examine the implications such mentality of self-centeredness or selfish interest will have on others.

Most people, especially those who have one emotional problem or the other value more the supportive presence of the caregivers than administrations of drugs or medications. Studies have proved that personal care has such therapeutic effects on people than the gifts of gold and silver. This is what has singled out Sullivan as the father of modern social psychiatry. The need to care more about the feelings of others is the springboard for effective psychiatry process and achievements. In a way, the theory of Sullivan's personality development is necessary for the study of psychology in general and the healing process of those I consider their lives hidden from others. Let people feel that you care for them first and they will eventually open up for you.

Therefore, the study of psychiatry that takes the comfort of the human person into serious consideration is the foundation stone of all studies and concerns about diagnoses, treatment and medication. The need for therapy in psychological practice cannot be overemphasized in handling mental cases. Thanks to nature, Sullivan delved into the field of social psychiatry by divine intervention. No wonder many people maintain that experience is the best teacher. In the light of this project, we shall continue to discuss Sullivan's interpersonal psychoanalysis in the order as outlined above:

B. Brief and informed summary of his life, education, and professional practice:

i. His birth:

He was born in the midst of emotional frustrations and what appeared regretful. Born on February 21, 1892, in a small village in New York State, grew under hard conditions. His parents, Timothy and Ella Stack Sullivan lost two sons before he was born. That meant that Harry Stack Sullivan had no siblings to play or interact with. That was the beginning of his early life story that later emerged him as a psychiatry expert of worth. Even his mother could not easily be consoled or bear the loss of such children she bore in her womb for 9 months each. The matter escalated to the point that, when Harry was three years, his mother disappeared for about a year and six months. In a way, Harry was more of a motherless baby. Had his maternal grandmother not initially cared for him, we could guess what could have happened to him? When the said grandmother died, another aunt came to raise him too. The experience of having three mothers at the same time, in today's society, meant he had no mother – passing from one cultural experience to the other. He had no friends, except one Clarence Bellinger. This childhood experience equally influenced his theories and convictions later in life. No wonder my people say, "Whatever way a tree bends, it falls in that direction"

ii. His Marriage/Religious status:

In actual fact, Sullivan did not marry but he adopted a young man who was regarded by his friends as his biological son. Regarding his religious preference, he was born into a Catholic family but never practiced it. He was more of anti-Catholic and non-religious too. But it was remarkable that he made a will to be buried as Catholic and that was granted him, postmortem. As nature would always take its course, Sullivan died on January 14, 1949, at the age of 57.

iii. <u>His education:</u>

As an intelligent young boy, his high marks at school set him apart from other students. His intelligence moved him away from farming work to University material. Hard work can be an asset to the achievements of high objectives in life. Sullivan proved this; call it a hypothesis, it is true. Because of his brilliance, he won a scholarship from the State of New York at the age of sixteen. Whether he graduated from the Chicago College without academic records as he intended was not the issue but his formidable strikes to achieve high education was unmatchable.

However, his failure to graduate in physics coupled with his hospitalization led him to a mental breakdown. By this time, Sullivan has consciously become a psychiatrist patient. He was not completely discouraged. He entered the school of medicine in 1911 and completed his studies in 1915. Not until two years later when he was able to pay for his school fees that he received his diploma. We can imagine what the situation meant for a student at that time, even today.

Fortunately, during his trying years of struggle, adjustments and speculations to become a man of worth, he was lucky to work with schizophrenic patients at various hospitals. It was an opportunity to come closer to others, listening to them and trying to understand their feelings. This was a way to interpersonal therapy. For him, "institutional environment was artificial and counterproductive to personality development" (Morgan, p.180). He served as a staff physician in the U.S. Army. Commenting on this experience, Helen Swick Perry said:

> *In his various published and unpublished writings, he describes with some delight his experience on the rifle range, when he stuck a "very, very dear friend of mine on one such occasions" with a pin when the friend was concentrating on firing. "And such enough, as I had expected, it was only after having fired that he reached around to the injured area and gave me the devil. Literally, on the rifle range, things are suspended from any disturbance of one's consciousness until it is time to notice them....Sullivan always told his story with humor and delight, as if the whole experience of the "young doctor" stationed on the Mexican border was a piece with nothing else up to that time (Helen Swick Perry, on the Life of Harry Stack Sullivan: p.167).*

When the William Alanson White Foundation was decided in 1939 that series of lectures be given in his honor, it was Sullivan that gave the first lecture, including four other lectures which he gave in small groups at the Department of the Interior in Washington, DC. It was at this period that he struggled to outline the concept of his personality development and psychiatric disorders and treatment. As luck had it, these lectures were published in 1940 at the journal, *"Psychiatry"* leading to the publication of his book – *Conceptions of Modern Psychiatry*, selling more than 13,000 copies in a short period of time. As we shall see later, this was where he defined the field of psychiatry, highlighting the need for psychology in society.

iv. <u>Professional Practice:</u>

Without any professional or previous training, he secured a position at St. Elizabeth's Hospital in Washington. He worked with a genius in the field of psychiatry like "Dr. William Alanson White, an early and successful psychiatrist trained in the Freudian school of psychoanalysis" (Morgan, p.181).

Besides, his clinical research at Sheppard and Enoch Pratt Hospital "consumed a portion of his life and passion from 1923 to 1930 and had a brief appointment in the University of Maryland's school of Medicine" (Ibid). It was at this time he seemed to have earned such a reputation in treating patients with schizophrenia and started to publish some materials on related areas.

These are evidences of the need for psychological practice in our time. This knowledge carried him to what he termed his "Baltimore period" of experimental developments. Based on his knowledge and experiences with schizophrenics, he started meditating on interpersonal relations as the basis and key ingredient in treating those characterized by impaired cognitive functional skills and behaviors – the mentally ill and intellectually disabled.

Eventually, he discovered that illness could be approached from non-medical means in terms of prescriptions. Therapeutic means is the key. Sullivan is credited for the distinction he made between cause and treatment of individuals with schizophrenic tendencies by insisting that social and interpersonal environments are fundamental in diagnosing and coping with mental cases than tracing them to biogenic origins, thereby supporting the target of this book.

In other words, the environments, associations and parental heredity easily influence and affect people. All the honest efforts we make to preserve and respect our environments lead to what I regard as "Eco-Spirituality" (Rev. Dr. Jude Osunkwo, PhD Thesis, 2012). Thus, the emphasis on spiritual psychology today is on this area of environment. Being sensitive to who we are, what we do and relate with others is foundational and defines us as rational beings. However, the emphasis Sullivan placed on social and interpersonal environments did not mean he had no regard for heredity. According to Helen Swick Perry, in support of Sullivan's stand, noted:

He is describing himself when he reports that 'people who have but limited ability for human intimacy can assuage loneliness through these instrumentalities [such as games and sports], without any risk of troublesome interpersonal developments (Helen, p.167).

In this sense, Sullivan implied that both in games and sports, human beings interact and engage in one activity or the other. No wonder in his definition of psychiatry, he noted that:

Psychiatry is the study of interpersonal relations. Psychiatry... is the study of processes that involve or go on between people. The field of psychiatry is the field of interpersonal relations, under any and all circumstances in which these relations exist (Harry Stack Sullivan, p. 240).

This observation is consequential and pertinent today; especially in a world some treat others as pieces of wood to be fixed. Sullivan is consistent in viewing the human person as precious and important institution to be respected and cared for. For instance, the American Heritage Dictionary and so many Dictionaries present and define psychiatry as: "The branch of medicine that deals with the diagnosis, treatment, and prevention of mental and emotional disorders" (American Heritage Dictionary of the English Language, 4th Edition).

Continuing on this analysis, Sullivan distinguished himself in this field by maintaining that: "As a preliminary analysis, one may divide human behavior, interpersonal relations, into two closely related kinds or categories, characterized by the pursuit of satisfactions and the pursuit of security" (Ibid). We shall discuss this aspect as part of the theories that have made him famous today. His professional practices will assist us understand, evaluate and underscore his theories the more, especially as they high-lighten the need for psychological practice or emotional healing of those afflicted with psychological problems.

    C. Key Theories that made him famous:

Sullivan is credited for his theory on personality development. Some of these theories have been noted already. But for the sake of emphasis, we shall present them in this order:

1. Interpersonal theory of Psychiatry:

According to Morgan, quoting Sullivan: "The concept of "personality" in itself is a hypothetical entity which cannot be isolated from interpersonal situations and, indeed, interpersonal behavior is all that is observable about a personality" (Morgan, p.184). This interpersonal behavior entails how we relate to one another and the effects of such relationships. According to the law of quantum physics, an observer cannot be separated from the experiences he or she is making. The study of personality has to do with the person in his concrete sense, his actions, behaviors, his aspirations and how far he goes to achieve them. In this sense, Sullivan appears to have merged the concept of psychiatry and psychology. People can only be defined by the ways they act and behave with others. In Morgan's presentation: "Modern psychiatry as defined and practiced by Sullivan consists of a study of personality characteristics which can be directly observed in the context of interpersonal relationships" (Morgan, p.185).

This recalls the relevance of Nwachukwu's book, the need to keep human relationships together is ontologically basic and a platitude. In Sullivan's understanding, personality characteristics extend to those activities by which we say this person is happy, sad, eating or doing this or that. Therefore, the value or relevance of psychology in society and individual lives cannot be overemphasized. It has created the awareness of interdependence and collaboration. For instance, when one yells at others without any reasons, the need for psychological consideration automatically arises as regards the best skills to address the issue.

2. <u>Basic Characteristics of Interpersonal relations:</u>

In this process, the first he identified was:

a. *Dynamism in personality theory.*

Sullivan believes that life is an on-going process that does not stop at nothing. There are flexibilities in human life. This process, for him, involves the following:
-The major characteristics that guide what man does which could be malevolence because of bad people in society,
-Lust which points to personal selfishness, and,
-Intimacy which is a positive dynamism that wishes the best of others.
By this awareness, each person is highly alerted to make the best course of life and decision.

b. *Personifications*

This may be counterproductive or profitable depending on the image one has formed about oneself and others. That is why people tend to address others as being good or bad, because they do this based on their personified thoughts. Yet, the best ways we can conceive others positively are by being objective and focused, not necessarily on peoples' bad qualities, but the honest efforts they make on daily basis.

c. Self-system:

This is the dynamism in personality structure. The self-system is the security measure or steps an individual takes to protect him or herself against possible anxieties and unpleasant situations. If people could realize this very value in their lives, this book would have achieved its objective. It was within this context that Sullivan spoke of pursuit of satisfactions and pursuits of security as we saw earlier. In his own words: "They explain why any situation in which two or more people are involved becomes an interpersonal situation".

Furthermore, it is because of these needs that "one cannot live and be human except in communal existence with others.... The pursuit of satisfactions is a response to primarily biological needs. Food and drink, sleep and rest, and the satisfaction of lust are all among them" (Harry Stack Sullivan, page Pp. 240 –241). In his understanding, the pursuit of security is culturally equipped. As one is born, one becomes conscious to live and interact with one's environments. Again, through psychology, humanity claims her prerogatives in preserving and protecting her environment in order to maximize it. By our being culturally equipped applies that without our environments, life is non-existent. That is why the pollution of the environment catastrophically leads to its own consequences.

Any movement that threatens this fundamental tendency has to be attacked by all means. For one to interact with others there must be environment that makes it possible or happen. It was also with this sense that Sullivan taught of "Power Motive" and "Power

Drive". In his analysis, each person is born with certain powers to communicate and live well with others. This does not mean power of governance, but of perseverance and ability to cope with life situations. On the other hand, power drive is acquired as one interacts in society. This drive assists one to overcome frustrated situations and respond positively to the happenings of life. [Consult, Harry Stack Sullivan, pages 242 – 244]. In self-system, the image you form of people is the way you intend to interact with them. In his own words: "As you judge yourself so shall you judge others" (Op. cit. p. 244). Therefore, to gain satisfactions and security is to have the power in every interpersonal relation. No one is insignificant in a relation. The process of integrating biological values and cultural ones is necessary in every interpersonal relation.

d. *Development of threefold classification of experiences*:

According to Sullivan in Morgan, "Experiences occur in three different modes" (Morgan, p.187):

> *The protaxic or prototaxic, parataxic and syntaxic. In the first one, experience is protaxic when it is based on imaginations without any real physical verifications, parataxic, when there are no logical connections between what appears to be the cause of an action and the actual context of proving it, and syntaxic way of thinking consists in logical reasoning and conclusions and "ability to predict causes from the knowledge of their effects (Ibid).*

All these theories tend to point at one thing: No one is an island. We need others to be human beings. Mere suspicion of other people's characters is nonsensical. It is only when we interact with people that we can say or tell who they are. At times, we become sick as the result of negative comments others make about or against us. Here lies the importance of this book – acquiring the ability to perceive ourselves as important and valuable documents of posterity irrespective of the ugly impressions others hold for us.

D. Analysis of Sullivan's work and its influence or relevance today:

Having presented the work and theories of Sullivan in a summary form, it is necessary to indicate their educational, social, religious, and psychological implications for the individuals reading this book in particular and society at large. It is easy for me to say and recommend the following, based on my understanding of Sullivan's ingenuity here:

➢ Nobody is an island unto him or herself. We need to understand that without human interpersonal relations, life becomes frustrating or boring. Sullivan experienced the loneliness of his family background and grew from its excruciating agony, hence the basis of his theories;

➢ Sullivan highlighted the importance of religion. Though, he did not claim to have practiced any, but he knew it was necessary to have one, hence he made a will to be buried as Catholic. In this way, he certified the authenticity, not only of Christianity but also of the Catholic Church;

➢ Human interactions and behaviors should be traced, not only from genes but to the environment in which one is raised and cultured;

➢ Life is empty without a relation in which each personality, those basic characteristics are noted. It is only when we know people and the stuff they are made of, that we can best interact and relate with them;

➢ Every life is as important as the other. There is no such thing for Sullivan as the superman. The need to pursue satisfaction and security is paramount and should not be limited to any individual person or persons;

➢ Education and high achievements depend on hard work and not necessarily on poor family background;

➢ The need to encourage the award of scholarships to brilliant children has been noted here by the personal life of Sullivan;

➢ The emphasis on psychiatry should include psychology because the manner in which a person with mental illness is approached is important too. Basically, psychiatry should be seen as involving the treatment of the whole person and not to limit it to any particular section. Hence, Sullivan recommended the need to involve therapy in treating mental cases;

➢ He differs from Freud in the sense that personality development should not hold any emphasis on sexual orientations but on the entire personality;

➢ The writing of Sullivan has supported my investigation on the necessity of healing that centers more on splinters and the root causes of problems, especially those associated with various emotions and feelings;

➢ Relationships should not be made professional but seen from the point of view of humanness. We need to relate as human being with same life goals and aspirations;

> There is no end to the advantages one can drive from Sullivan's theories. For any study of human personality that does not involve the entire person, his actions, feelings, preoccupations etc, should be discarded;

> Psychiatry should not be limited to medicine alone, the manner in which professionals approach their client matters too, in their healing process.

There are as many psychoanalysts as there are various branches of psychology. In our study of Sullivan's system of education, psychiatry should be fundamentally integrative of social aspects of life. Every emphasis should be laid on the person on the moment. Speculation is an aspect of philosophy. In the present situation or studies, there is no room for such theories that have no application in concrete human situation.

Life is basically relations, whether with a psychiatry case or normal person. The need to have self-system that assists one make good judgments is necessary. If you are unreliable, Sullivan tells you to self-supervise and try to remove the plank in your own eyes first before you can pass such negative judgments on others.

I really appreciate the exposure my research or book has brought to me through my studies at Graduate Theological Foundation, which is in line with Sullivan and Morgan's aims at offering the best educational opportunity to humanity. At this juncture therefore, we shall try to study and examine the work of other Psychologists who have made tremendous impacts in the field of psychological practice and psychotherapy.

F. ERIK ERIKSON AND DEVELOPMENTAL PSYCHOLOGY

1. Brief summary of his life, education and achievement

2. His key Concepts and Theories

3. Evaluation of his theories and influence on society

Introduction:

We have so much to say here. Thus, we may not strictly adhere to one formula. The life of Erik Erikson is a demonstration of the value of psychology, especially in the hidden lives of human beings. It is true that Erik Erikson is one of the leading authorities on human development. His teaching and insights in interdependent education on individual growth, historical change and famous concepts have not only challenged the ways many perceive themselves today but also changed their behaviors.

Therefore, in writing a book on a famous psychologist such as Erik Erikson, I am bound to substantiate my position and analysis of this great man based on his writings himself and what other influential authors have said about him. This is the high water mark of scholarship. Erik essentially followed the argument of Sigmund Freud in his personality development, with some differences. The need to understand today the development of an individual cannot be overemphasized in that development is a process that begins from birth till death. In other to justify our claims, we shall first of all discuss his life, education and part of the achievements he made as a hard working psychologist and psychotherapist.

1. Brief summary of Erik's life, education and achievements

  i. Birth:

Erik Homburger was born on June 25, 1902 in Germany. His mother, Karla Abrahamsen, a Jewish woman hailed from a very prominent family. His father, Erik Salomonsen deserted his mother even before he was born. Luckily, before he was born his mother had got remarried to one Jewish stockbroker, Waldemar Isidor Salomonsen, a name with which he was officially at that time registered in German.

His mother was trained as a nurse and later, in 1904, remarried to a physician named Dr. Theodor Hombuger. The doctor was an American, who was, as of that time, serving as his own pediatrician doctor and in 1911, he officially adopted him; hence his official name became Hombuger. However, when Erik fled from Germany and arrived the United States as his homeland, he changed his surname to Erikson after obtaining his U. S. citizenship. According to Morgan:

> *Personal, racial, and religious identity seemed to have plagued Erikson from his earliest memories and haunted him throughout his childhood, adolescent and adult life. It has been suggested that possibly this life experience itself was a significant ingredient in leading him to the development of his now famous eight stages of development" (Morgan, 2010:133 – 134).*

ii. Education

Erik's primary interest was in arts but eventually his burning passion for psychology motivated him to the field of psychoanalysis. He engaged and studied at a variety of places in Germany before settling to the discipline of his heart desire. He did not initially obtain formal educational training beyond high school diploma besides his confidence and insights into the areas of his interest. He attended a humanistic gymnasium but did not do well there till he distinguished himself in ancient history and art as against his stepfather's urgings to do medicine. It was on account of his interest in art that he traveled across central Europe to satisfy his heart desires.

In his ceaseless efforts to find the best educational opportunity, he left Europe at a time and went back to Germany to study at the famous art school, the Dunst-Akademia. Two years later, he went to Florence all in search for his educational goals. As luck would have it, in 1927 when he was 25 years of age, he got a teaching appointment "at an experimental school for wealthy American children living with their parents in Vienna" (Ibid).

The school, Kinderseminar under the directorship of Dorothy Burlingham, was aimed at assisting American professionals studying in Vienna to become psychoanalysts. Erik capitalized and cashed in at that opportunity, underwent psychoanalysis and was introduced to the Montessori education method and to Anna Freud, who had been team worker to Dorothy Burlingham. From here, "Erik was introduced and welcomed to Vienna Psychoanalytic Society which was Sigmund Freud's teaching and training psychoanalysis to medical professionals and selected layman alike" (Op. cit. 2010:135).

As a very brilliant scholar, he taught at this very Anna Freud and Dorothy Burglingham's experimental school at Vienna. In the words of Morgan:

> Besides undergoing psychoanalysis at the hands of Anna Freud herself, Erikson also took the Certificate from the Maria Montessori Teachers Association in Vienna, his own academic credential throughout his whole professional life. (Ibid).

These brands of studies were the springboards for fostering his passion for analytical studies in childhood maturation. From his own professional experiences and fieldworks, Erikson developed his ideas and theories on human personality development.

iii. Marriage life

In 1929, Erikson married an American teacher and dancer, Joan Serson, who was at the time of marriage a member of the same Anna Freud's and Dorothy Burlingham's experimental school in Vienna. According to Morgan:

> By 1933, they had two sons and the whole Erikson family then attempted to emigrate to Copenhagen where he had hoped to secure citizenship based upon his natural father's nationality (Ibid).

Erikson and his family migrated to the University of California in the US at Berkeley in 1939 where he intensified his search on child welfare and personality development and practiced as a clinical psychologist at the San Francisco Veterans Hospital. There he treated people with trauma and mental illness as a psychotherapist too. It was sad to note that: "Erikson died in Harwick, Massachusetts, May 12, 1994" (Ibid). That was the time his Canadian wife, Joan whom he married as a young teacher in Vienna joined in his academic mission.

Joan herself was an academic and was so interested in her husband's field of research, namely childhood development and went ahead with her husband's research and publications. In all, the couples had three sons and one daughter. Unfortunately one of his sons, Neil by name was permanently institutionalized in a prestigious public hospital for mentally retarded children as an infant from Down syndrome child. As Lawrence J. Friedman puts it: "Joan spent the full morning describing the course of the tragedy of her Down syndrome child" (Friedman, 215). This was a turning point in the marriage life of Erikson, which nearly broke their marriage. The condition of such a child made them feel so humiliated that most often they were in denial that there was no such child. They even lied to their other children that Neil died at birth, what a disturbing and frustrating situation.

It was at a later time in years that the older son was told the truth of the whereabouts of the said child. The other children became cognizant of the true story after Neil had eventually died. Joan later in life blamed herself for not taking any photos of Neil and the ways they seemed to keep aloof or take a distance from the poor sick child. Efforts to close up the reality of such a child hit at the center of their marriage. When the family moved back to New England, it was the time that Erikson informed his other children of a brother whose condition made it impossible to join them. There was no time his other siblings set their eyes on their brother, Neil. It seemed unbelievable and frightened Erikson's daughter. However, Neil lived up to twenty-two years old before he died in 1965. This time, the couple, Erikson and his wife were absent, living in Europe. It was from there that they called their other son and daughter living by then in California to arrange for the burial of Neil, their brother. As it were, none of them, Erikson and his wife came home for the burial.

Since psychoanalytic practice was not well known in Denmark, Erikson had hoped or wanted to establish it there, but luck was not in his favor. Besides, due to Hitler's regime he was afraid to proceed with his plans and left the area. It was on the same year that he completed a course of study at the Vienna Psychoanalytic Institute.

iv. Career

When Erik moved to the US in 1933, he had wonderful opportunities at some of America's most distinguished centers of learning. These included Harvard University, Yale and the University of California located at Berkeley. As soon as he arrived Boston in 1933, "he set up as one of the very few child psychoanalysts in the country and carried out research on children at the prestigious Harvard psychological Clinic where he enjoyed a close relationship with both Henry Murray and Kurt Lewin" (Op. Cit. 136). He was eventually appointed as a clinical and academic Research Fellow in Psychology in the Department of Neuropsychiatry at Harvard Medical School, from 1933 to 1935. From 1936 to 1939, he served another appointment in the Department of Psychiatry in the Institute of Human Relations at Yale University Medical School. Erikson was so happy to work there especially in his continuing work and interest in personality development and cross-cultural studies.

Erik had concentrated on integrating and extending Freud's theories on psychoanalysis and carry them out or test them within the areas of social and cultural factors and how the influence human development and personality. He was particularly fascinated about how society affects childhood and its development, agreeing with Sullivan's perspective on human development. This was the core of his research. His interest in this area of multi-cultural studies of childhood and society led him into studying cultural anthropology, essentially as it relates to the study of children, societal effects on them and personality development cross-culturally. In the words of Morgan:

> To deepen his understanding of cross-culturalism and child development, he journeyed to the Native American communities of the Oglala Lakota (Sioux) and the Yurok peoples where he stayed for extended times of observation, interviews, etc (Ibid).

The riches of this fieldwork and the experiences energized his ambitions and convictions above the researches of other psychologists. His cross-cultural experiences were turning points on his insistency regarding the dynamics of children's developmental histories, especially on childhood and society. He moved to the people, the society itself and observed for himself what goes on in them. He became convinced of his research focus and ambitious achievements. Having migrated to California at Berkeley as noted already, made every effort to develop his child welfare and personality development. By 1942, he had risen to the position of a professor of psychology at the University of California in Berkeley where he assisted Jean MacFarlane in the Child Guidance Study. Because he did not want to sign a loyalty oath during McCarthy era, unlike today that the practice is required by law for all teachers, he moved back to Massachusetts.

As history would have it, in 1951, Erikson had joined a group of mental health professionals at the Austen Riggs Center in Stockbridge, Massachusetts, which was a private residential treatment center for mentally ill young people. Erikson was so versatile, maintaining a part-time teaching appointment at the Western psychiatric Institute in Pittsburgh, Pennsylvania while also teaching at the University of Pittsburgh and Massachusetts Institute of technology. From 1951–1960, he taught and worked in New England, but in the summer of 1960, he did Advanced Studies of the Behavioral Sciences at Palo Alto, California and was "rewarded the following year to teach at Harvard University from where he retired in 1970 from his clinical practice but concentrated on writing" (Confer Morgan, 2010:137).

v. Achievements

The publication of his first book in 1950 titled "*Childhood and Society*" was revolutionary in academics. Here Erikson has proved to the world the relationship that constantly and naturally exists between society and the development of children or their personality development. He elaborated what he referred to as "triple bookkeeping". He insisted that the understanding or behavior of any person involves certain factors, namely "somatic, social context, and ego development, each in relation to the other" (Op. Cit. 2010:139 –140). In doing this, he substantially made references to Freudian theories of psychosexual development. His cross-cultural analysis assisted in underscoring the need or power of social context in relation to child – rearing practices and their effects on later personality development. The three processes of personality development, somatic, social context and ego development are interdependent and each is relative and relevant to the other. In other words, without their symbiotic corporation and teamwork, there cannot be a reliable personality development.

This stand or position was an edge over the traditional position of Freud on his personality development and child sexuality – the id, ego and superego. By this position Erikson has not only elaborated on the theory of psychosexual developments as produced by Freud but also modified them. The role culture and society play in the child – rearing cannot be overemphasized – the anthropological and social context analysis. In the words of Morgan:

> *A fundamental component of Erikson's theory of ego development is the assumption that development of the person is marked by a series of stages that are universal to humanity (Op. Cit. 140).*

While there are truths in the claims Erikson has made, the claims are subject to further investigations since cultures differ because what is considered as an atrocity or evil in one culture may be welcomed as a grace in another. That means, there cannot be any universal agreement in culture and behaviorisms. However, the fact that there are some forces or genetic values transmitted from parent to children remains an unbeatable point Erikson has made. There is another point, which I share with Erikson in the sense that in each stage of a child's development and life, there are some crisis or critical turning points arising from physiological maturation and social demands made upon the person at each stage is true for me. In other words: "The various components of personality are, in his theory, determined by the manner in which each of these crises are resolved" (Op. Cit. 141).

The issue of making conflict a vital and integral part of his theory is necessary due to the happenings in life today. For instance, what one considers beautiful from the outside may turn ugly inside and so on – concurring with the paradoxical co-existence of good and evil of Heraclitus and Paul Tillich? This is an anticipated crisis that assists society move on with life and not of war fares or catastrophes.

2. Erik's key Concepts and Theories

With the psychosocial growth of the ego, Erikson becomes one of the leading psychologists working in the area of personality development like Freud and the rest of them. The fact of ego is central in both Freud and Erikson. But what this ego stands for, differs from both Psychologists. While Freud appropriated ego as part of the fundamental structures of personality, Erikson presented it as autonomously the center of human personality development. Again, Erikson presented ego as the main source from which its relationships with parents, and socio-historical matrix within the family life [in which the child's ego or power to live or die] develops. In Freud's view, the ego develops, but in Erikson, "ego development theory covers the entire span of psychological growth throughout the individual's life" (Op. Cit. 143).

As noted already, the basis of Erikson's position is that the "development of the individual is marked by a series of "stages" that are universal to every person throughout the world" (Ibid). And each of these stages of development carries with it a "crisis" that is, a critical turning point as noted already, in the individual's life that arises from physiological maturation and social demands made upon the person at that very stage. In Erikson's view, this very component of each person's personality could be positive or negative, depending on the basis on which it is developed. Based on this dialectic nature of each person's development in Erikson's analysis, I have chosen to discuss his theories right in this section.

The eight stages of man in his developments in Erikson:

a. Basic Trust vs. Basic Mistrust

According to Erikson in `Childhood and Society: *The first demonstration of social trust in the baby is the ease of his feeding, the depth of his sleep, the relaxation of his bowls. The experience of a mutual, regulation of his increasingly receptive capacities with the maternal techniques of provision gradually helps him to balance the discomfort caused by the immaturity homeostasis with which he was born (Erik Erikson, in Morgan, 2010:247).*

There is trust or confidence in the child when the atmosphere he is enjoying continues in the same magnitude with which it started. The child feels confidence on himself with the first one year. But where these basic amenities provided him by the mother or baby setting are lacking, the child begins to feel the sense of mistrust and whatever way he feels affects his later personality development in life. For Erikson, each stage is interconnected with the next stage.

b. Autonomy vs. Shame and Doubt

From the age of 2 to 3 years, if the child really enjoyed the previous stage of trust, he begins to feel autonomous on what he can do himself. He wants to feed himself directly from the table. In

Erikson's own words, the child wants to have will power "to let pass and to let be" (Op. Cit. 251). He wants to take pride in accomplishing something himself. However, where the society makes it impossible to achieve his desires, be it his mother or relation, he begins to feel the sense of shame and also doubt his ability to live or not. This is the very crisis Erik is talking about.

c.   Initiative vs. Guilt

When the child turns 3 to 5 years, he begins to explore reality himself. In Erikson's own words, "There is in every child at every stage a new miracle of vigorous unfolding, which constitutes a new hope and a new responsibility for all" (Op. Cit. 255). This stage can only be so if the criteria for development are the same at all times and seasons. If the goals the child has contemplated for him-self is stifled by society or family, and does not accomplish them, then he develops the sense of guilt. That is why society is encouraged to assist the child achieve its objectives in life.

d.   Industry vs. Inferiority

This is within the ages of 6 to 11, the latency age of Freud. This is the age the child is set to enter into life, including school life and peer groupings. According to Erikson, the child "must begin to be a worker and a provider" (Op. Cit. 259), forgetting past hopes and aspirations that were not accomplished and begin to try different industries or works. The playtime is over. For the child "to bring a productive situation to completion is an aim which gradually supersedes the whims and wishes of play" (Ibid). At this stage, his ego boundaries include his tools and skills, the work principles. Here the child begins to develop his technological aptitude for exploration. Within these technological advancements, there arises crisis when these wonderful goals are obstructed by the course of events in life. He feels high before his peers and inferior once he feels disappointed in life.

e. Identity vs. Role Confusion

As an adolescent, he begins to take note of the class he belongs and proves his worth there. This is the time of youthful age or stage. In his own words, "With the establishment of a good initial relationship to the world of skills and tools, and with the advent of puberty, childhood proper comes to an end" (Erikson, 261).

However, this stage cannot be worthwhile if the previous stages were not well resolved or formed the foundation for this present one. That is why Erikson made this elaborate statement:

> *The growing and developing youths, faced with this physiological revolution within them, and with tangible adult tasks ahead of them are now primarily concerned with what they appear to be in the eyes of others as compared with what they feel they are, and with the question of how to connect the roles and skills cultivated earlier with the occupational prototypes of the day (Ibid).*

This is what brings about the role confusion. The ability to balance what the youth thinks he can accomplish, his identity and how the society is going to evaluate and criticize him brings about confusion in his roles as youth. Intolerance may lead to a defense of one's identity and thereby creating the crisis in question.

f. Intimacy vs. Isolation

Once the youth has identified himself in society, that forms the basis to establish some intimacy with her – "the capacity to commit himself to concrete affiliations and partnerships and to develop the ethical strength to abide by such commitments, even though they may call for significant sacrifices and compromises" (Op. Cit. 263). This is where the body and ego come together to shape the societal expectations. But where and when these set objectives to form intimacy seem obstructed, the youth either isolates himself from such stimuli or fight to destroy them completely to maintain one's identity and enjoy the intimacy.

g. Generativity vs. Stagnation

As an adult, the individual who has fully enjoyed some intimacy in society wants to make contributions to the world. In this sense, generativity is more of productivity and creativity. In his own words, according to Erikson, "Mature man needs to be needed, and maturity needs guidance as well as encouragement from what has been produced and must be taken care of" (Op. Cit.267). The full mature man must leave a legacy to be emulated by youngsters. In an elaborate sense:

> Generativity thus is and essential stage on the psychosexual as well as on the psychosocial schedule. Where such enrichment fails altogether, regression to an obsessive need for pseudo-intimacy takes place, often with a pervading sense of stagnation and the personal impoverishment (Ibid).

Each of these stages affects each other in a very drastic manner. As already noted above, failure to achieve one's set objectives in one stage, leads to disappointments in others and vice versa.

h. Ego Integrity vs. Despair

According to Erik, "Only in him who in some way has taken care of things and people and has adapted himself to the triumphs and disappointments adherent to being, the originator of others or the generator of produces and ideas – only in him may gradually ripen the fruit of these seven stages. I know no better word for it than ego integrity (Op. Cit. 268). Ego integrity is the summary of what it means to be a full responsible person, who is aware of himself and his environments. But we know from what happens in actual life situations, no one is an island, most often things do not go the ways we want them, and such brings about the despair in question.

Eventually, having examined the major theories of Erikson, especially the eight stages of human development, I shall now, discuss and present the impacts of the teachings for others and me in general.

3. Evaluation of theories and impacts on individuals

This is going to be my conclusion in this section as well. I shall try and present these educational implications in a summary fashion and in this order:

a. From my studies of Erikson, I am beginning to question myself if I have actually made the best use of my life. How far has my profession influenced others today?

b. People need to count more on their own achievements in life than hoping for others to decide for them how to live their lives;

c. With Erikson's theories, the need to persevere in doing that which is noble or best, is necessary;

d. As one begins to enjoy one's life to the full, there is need also to be aware that there could be obstacles on the way, which might make it impossible to reach the end of it;

e. Creativity is important in life. Even taking initiative without being policed about is important too;

f. From Erikson's position, every family should always plan ahead of them, imagining what will happen when a family member dies and how to get about dealing with it;

g. Erikson has employed such ethical principles and values like integrity, industry, initiative, intimacy and autonomy in one's field of specializations;

h. There is need for one to know ahead of time how others will reflect upon one's actions and that will help one to behave better;

i. More importantly, I am who I am, what I want to achieve and who I want to become, not because I am alone in society, but because I have made up my mind to succeed in life irrespective of the crisis of life;

j. Crisis is inevitable, but the ability to handle it is wisdom.

Erikson's teachings, though some seem exaggerated, there are needs to examine them closely for healing opportunities. He made a substantial comparison of Freud's analysis of human development. While Freud presents the individual to grow from the id, ego and superego, Erik centers his emphasis on the ego. We can here understand that Erikson was not a moral psychologist from the point of view of Freud who saw the moral arms of society in his superego. Finally, people can criticize Erikson because of most of his big claims and generalizations, his teachings are important today for a selfish world like ours where many people constitute obstacles for the achievements of others. Let people be allowed to find where they fit or belong and be useful to society at large. With Erik's psychological input, people are hereby prepared to expect the unexpected when things do not go the ways they want them and move forward to enjoy their lives. It was basically from this point of view that I examined the life and work of Adler Alfred.

G. APPLICATION OF ALFRED ADLER'S INDIVIDUAL PSYCHOLOGY TO EVERYDAY LIFE

A. Introduction

B. Brief Summary of Adler's life, education and key achievements

C. His key concepts and theories

D. Evaluation and application of his theories and influences on society

A. Introduction

I am particularly delighted to study Alfred Adler for his new approach to psychology in general and theory of human personality due to my set objectives on this book and the best possible manners I can assist others in need. So many experts have developed one aspect of the theory of human personality or the other. In a very remarkable manner, Alfred Adler has singled himself out to be one of the founding fathers of "individual psychology" because of his originality in this field. As the theme suggests, any study or program on psychology that does not take the interest of the individual as its primary focus is bound to fail or lead to a wrong priority. However, in this book, I am going to apply Alfred Adler's teachings on a collectivist culture as it affects the individual, especially like the Igbo of Nigeria, where the individual appears to submerge in the community consciousness, which sounds more of a communist system. There is need to situate this book on the context of 'who a person is' and what makes him grow.

In the case of the Igbo people of Nigeria, they have a system of community consciousness. The lives of the people are viewed from a common background so that whatever happens to an individual is considered as happening to every member of the community. From Adler's theories where the individual is at the helm of affairs, the community control of the individual might seem affected. However, when we consider Adler's understanding of society or environment and the role it plays in the life and development of a child, there are areas of agreement that can fit in both positions – Adler and the Igbo people of Nigeria. Before we can effectively draw a conclusion on the position Alder is holding as regards the theory of human psychology as it affects the development of a child, it is important we study his background first. Every emphasis made here is intentional.

B. Brief Summary of Adler's life, education and key achievements

i. Family Life:

Alfred Adler was born on February 7, 1870 into a Jewish family of Leopold Beer and Pauline Beer. He was a contemporary of Sigmund Freud, who happened to be his elderly brother. They have influential theories on human personality. While Freud extensively developed his own theory within the area of psychoanalysis, Adler built his own within the area of Psychosocial perspective. Their varying philosophical positions are going to color this writing in a remarkable manner. They lived with their parents in the village of Rudolfsheim, near the suburb of Vienna. According to Adler, as quoted in Dr. Morgan: "These were happy days for Adler as he says" (Morgan, 2010:51):

> As far as I can look back, I was always surrounded by friends and comrades, and for the most part, I was a well-loved playmate. This development began early and has never ceased. It is probably this feeling of solidarity with others that my understanding of the need for cooperation arose, a motive which has become the key to Individual Psychology (Adler in Morgan, Ibid).

From the above quotation we can deduce the therapeutic role his surroundings played in his life, hence the choice of his anthropological visions in his individual psychology. However, it is important that towards his adulthood, Adler missed such warmth of relationships and friendliness. The influence external environments have on individuals, to great portion, assists in determining their style of life, as we shall see later in this book. Because Adler lost his little brother, Rudolf, he developed interest in medicine as a way of dealing with sick people. Even though young Adler as of that time did not fancy Jewish religion, he found Biblical stories very interesting, and eventually ended up as a Protestant.

ii. Career/Education:

His elderly brother's approach to philosophy of life shaped his own way of thinking. In 1888, he graduated from the Nernals Gymnasium and at 18 years of age, he was accepted into the University of Vienna's school of medicine, a course of study he completed within 7 years. Unfortunately, he came out with lowest possible grades from the school of medicine. However, as Austria-Hungarian citizen, he officiated as a volunteer medical worker in a free medical hospital, Viennese Polinik. This was the period he got involved in social activities and later joined the Social Democratic Party. It was on record, that his elderly brother, Freud made the economic life of the entire family comfortable.

In 1897, for the first time in his life, according to sources, Adler fell in love with Raissa T. Epstein and that was all we knew how they marriage started. His wife was equally a Jew, born in Moscow, into an affluent Jewish family, attended the University of Zurich, did Biology, Zoology, and wanted to have a degree in natural sciences. At the age of 27 and 24, respectfully, two of them got married at the city of Russia on December 23, 1897. Their families were fully in support of it. It was clear; both missed their cherished family members. After the wedding they returned to Vienna for Adler's medical practice and after one year of the wedding, Raissa gave birth to their first baby, Valentine Dina. As luck had it, this time, Adler's medical practice grew by leaps and bounds and this was the time he began working on his theories on "inferiority, compensation, and overcompensation". At the age of 28, Adler published his first series of scholarship article, into a monograph entitled 'Health Book for the Tailor Trade'. Here, he reflected his passion for the working-class medical conditions. This very concern characterized his entire professional career, as we shall see later.

All these years, Adler virtually lost contact with his two brothers and two sisters. Even Raissa, his wife experienced the same loss of family warmth and interactions. However, Adler would often come in contact with his elderly brother, Freud because they practiced medicine and psychiatry at Vienna. At one point, Adler was asked to join his brother's Wednesday Psychological Society as the youngest member of this small group of young psychiatrists and physicians.

In 1904, Adler published an important article entitled: "The Physician as Educator" with emphasis on the physician role as 'a preventer rather than a curer" of children with special mental cases and illness. It was this very year that Adler got converted to Protestantism with his daughters without any stress on fanaticism. As we shall study in his theories, he shifted his emphasis from Freud's position on "sexual gratification" as the basis for human personality development to "drive for assertion". Adler believed that life is an on-going process that has many factors that affect its growth or deterioration. That was why he founded more of his own independent Society for Free Psychoanalytic Study than the rigid Psychoanalysis Society of Freud at Vienna.

From his psychoanalytical studies, he preferred deprivation as a form of punishment than physical beating or hitting. His series of teachings assisted him greatly. While in America, in 1912, he published his "The Neurotic Constitution" whereby, mental illness has to be addressed from the point of experience. In the next two years, he joined his colleagues to publish their "Journal for Individual Psychology" which was the beginning of the development of his school of psychotherapy called "Individual Psychology". Of course, this movement of Adler did not please Freud in his "Psychosexual personality development".

Man cannot be reduced to instinct as Freud would want us believe. Hoffman Edward quoting and commenting on the position of Adler in contradistinction with Freud citied Adler saying: "Just as we do not want to identify individual psychology with those parts of psychoanalysis that we believe are mistaken --- we would not want to burden the psychoanalytic school with discoveries which must appear heretical" (Hoffman Edward, forwarded by Kurt A. Adler, 2010:122). Though, Freud had acquired fame and money from his position in these theories of human developments, but Adler advocated, "social feeling" as the basis for individual psychology which incorporates compassion, altruism, and selflessness" (Op. Cit p.51).

Having seen that the effects of the World War 1 brought elements of socialism, Adler condemned 'capitalism' out rightly because it is "inequitable in the distribution of goods and services"(Adler in Morgan, p. 56). The human nature has its capacity to fight repulsive impulses or external aggressions. Thus, in 1920, he published his collection of essays designed to establish individual psychology as a school of thought in psychotherapy, entitled "The Practice and Theory of Individual Psychology". This publication made him famous both in Europe and America as a strong allay to child psychology. No wonder, in 1924, he was made "a professor of psychology with special interests in child developmental and educational psychology at the Pedagogical Institute's Division of Remedial Education" (Op. Cit. p.57).

In America for instance, Individual Psychology became welcoming news. For him, two factors affect all human relations, namely, the inferiority complex and the striving for social feelings"(Ibid) or social interests, leading to the publication of his most famous book, the "Understanding of Human Nature". The news of this new psychology was even carried and published in New York Times. Adler advocates for individual strength to overcome inadequacies in human nature and strive with the latent good inherent in nature to fight it – inferiority complex. Never give up in fighting for your survival. There are so many hatred, backsliding, backbiting, envy, jealousy, and problems of disharmony and maladjustment resident in human nature, in society and among people. Individual psychology, for Adler, "can cure individuals of the evil effects of this sense of inferiority" (Op. Cit. p. 58), and strive ahead to rule the world. In this sense, inferiority could be channeled and "developed into powerful instrument for ridding nations and groups of the menace of their collective inferiority complex" (Ibid). He emphasized this inferiority as being central in his understanding of human nature.

It is only when one has admitted that one has a problem that a sort of solution can be sought. According to Adler cited in Morgan, "The behavior pattern of persons, can be studied from their relation to three things: to society, to work, to sex" (Adler in Morgan, p. 59), corresponding to the great issues a person faces in life, namely occupation, society, and love. The role of parents and teachers, for instance, is to assist the "child to create a style of life that is profitable for him-self, for society, and for posterity" (Ibid). The emphasis is far beyond one aspect of a person. Adler took the development of all the aspects of the child into consideration. This has made him special. He never stopped talking of the need to "stimulate in the child a sense of confidence, to evoke his cooperative dispositions, to socialize and humanize his ego, especially to teachers and parents" (Ibid). In sharp contrast with his brother, Freud who presented man as a "so constructed by nature that he wishes only to satisfy his drives", Adler maintained in Individual Psychology that, "The development of the individual, because of his bodily inadequacy and his feeling of inferiority, is dependent on society. Hence, social feeling is inherent in man and is bound up with his identity" (Op. Cit, p. 60).

In a more practical and elaborate manner, Adler remarks, "The most important single factor in personality development is the relative presence of the inferiority complex.... This feeling of inferiority forms the background for all our studies. It ultimately becomes the stimulus among all individuals, whether children or adults, to establish their actions in such a way that they will arrive at a goal of superiority" (Ibid). After having returned to New York in 1929 to promote his latest book, "The Technique of Individual Psychology", he died of heart attack at the age of 67 years. We are going to continue with the clarification of his key concepts and theories.

C. His key concepts and theories

The major difference between Adler and Freud is on their theory of human personality development. Freud seemed to be carried away by his emphasis on sexuality, which for him is the basis of human personality development. For him, sexual conflicts in early childhood caused mental illness, psychotic or neurotic disorders. But for Adler, while he believes that sexuality has great role to play in human personality development, it does not fundamentally form the basis, rather it plays an important role in the whole process of human strivings to overcome that basic feeling of inadequacy or inferiority complex inherent and resident in every person from birth. That was the point Adler made in his book, entitled, "Understanding Human Nature" published in 1927, which has made him famous today in the field of psychotherapy.

As it were, according to him as cited in Morgan, "This book is an attempt to acquaint the general public with the fundamentals of Individual Psychology. At the same time it is a demonstration of the practical application of these principles to the conduct of one's everyday relationships, not only to the world, and to one's fellowmen, but also to the organization of one's personal life" (Op. Cit. p. 62). According to Adler, the main purpose of this masterpiece is to educate the general public how an individual's mistake can affect the harmony of the entire society and communal life system. In order words, the individual must recognize his mistakes, learn from and use them to effect a harmonious adjustment to the communal life. This is a system of thought that should be trumpeted in our time where nobody seems to take note of his or her mistakes. Instead, some people brag with their mistakes and wish to force them on others too.

Eventually, this thought led him to the conclusion that before we judge people, it is necessary we understand and know the situation in which they grew up and that was what he termed "The Family

Constellation" or Birth Order of each child. It is important to know if an individual is a first-born, an only child, the youngest child or the life wire because a child's birth order plays a major role in his character, behavior or life style. The manner in which the family may view these orders could affect the life of the child. At times, parents tend to ascribe qualities based on the above fact. For instance, "My baby is the best". Such appellations for Adler do not encourage any child to be holistic and harmonious in behavior. It is more of a lavished priority. Progress, peace and happiness do not consist on being the first, the only child or the youngest. When people or parents think along that way, they make such children one-sided in behavior and pompous and encourage them to look down on others. It is better we allow each child discover his inadequacies and fight them than praising them to their doom. If not, they become mere "alibi artist" who attempts nothing useful, but spends his whole energy wasting time...always finding excuses for his failures" (Op. Cit. p. 64). This birth order plays major role in Adler's child psychiatry – mental development because each order has its peculiarities that might affect the personality development of that child if not properly handled.

Consequently, the position a child occupies in a family shapes and colors his natural instincts, tropisms, and faculties which he brings into the world at birth. It does not matter what circumstances a child is exposed to, the most important urge is to strive ahead to surmount those obstacles. Each child has the natural power to forge ahead and be useful. In this instance, while Freud places this natural propensity on "will to pleasure", Adler pillows them on "will to power" as the driving force for a child's superiority over his peers. In this sense, he advocates that the social environment, particularly the parents and educators should assist in shaping the child's future. Once an individual develops the social feeling, social interest, then, he channels his powers to societal advancements, the developmental obstacles placed on each child notwithstanding. That is why Morgan observes, "Adler is eager for the informed parent and educational system to be aware of the drive or will to power which characterizes human nature and the absolute necessity of guiding and educating that drive for the welfare of human society" (Op. Cit. p. 66).

D. Evaluation and application of his "Theories" and influences on society

We are studying his theories vis-à-vis their application in human actions. As such, I shall present and treat the key operating phrases and words in his theory, in this order:

Compensation:

This was a later development in his treatment of human personality growth. He believed that the overriding motivation in most individuals is a striving for superiority because of their inherent inferiority complex. Later, he modified this conception to mean that people compensate themselves by building up feelings that work against inferiority. A good example of compensational behavior is appearing very neat and well dressed in the midst of dignitaries, where one, could not have naturally featured. This feeling starts from early childhood for self-realization, completeness and perfection. On the other hand, this very quest to be somebody big is usually being "frustrated by the feelings of inadequacy, incompleteness and inferiority arising from physical defects, low social status, pampering or neglect during childhood etc" (Op. Cit. P. 67).

In a way, compensational behavior, against or relative to these feelings of inadequacy, can result to the development of personal skills and abilities to fight them. However, "Overcompensation" for inferiority feelings can lead to unnecessary competitions, striving for power and self-aggrandizement that limit others' values and freedom. For instance, instead of doing that which is noble and self-satisfying, one goes ahead to add certain behaviors to show others of one's power and superiority, leading to "will to pleasure" instead of "will to power". By this etiological discovery, Adler has become world renowned for his creative and innovative response to the need for the cultivation and monitoring of mental health, particularly among children.

Relationship:

For Adler, there is direct relationship that exists between each person and the world around him because of certain biological principles in human nature. For example, most often, laughter is a sign of joy and tears indicate sorrow or afflictions. Thus, psychoneurosis (mental illness) is perceived as a distraction between the individual and his social environment. We see this happen among parents who have mentally ill children. Adler, instead of agreeing with Freud that man is motivated by instincts, he holds that man is motivated by social urges – to be with others, learn their language, and be useful to them. This theory led him to his teaching on "creative self". That is why "Individual Psychology is built upon the notion of a fundamental unity of the human personality. All the apparent dichotomies and multiplicities of life are organized in one self-consistent totality. ...No definite division can be made between mind and body, consciousness and unconsciousness, or between reason and emotion. All behavior is seen in relation to the final goal of superiority or success of the will to power" (Op. Cit. p. 69).

Creative Self:

Because, man by nature is interpersonal, requiring cooperation of others in social activities, then he seeks for "social interest or social feeling". In a more direct manner, it is within human nature that each human being is so highly personalized, subjective individual; he always interprets his social environment and tries to figure out well the best manner to utilize it for his survival and betterment. This idea of Adler is new in the field of psychoanalysis and psychotherapy. While Freud and his school of thought believe that personality relies more on inborn instincts for self-aggrandizement, Adler believes that the human person seeks for experience – with society, parent and teachers, as an aid towards his self-fulfillments in life. He maintains that man is absolute uniqueness of his personality. It was within this context that Adler noted: "Each person is a composite of his own personalized motivations, traits, interests, and values and each person, then, carries a distinctive style of life unique to his experiences and situation in the social environment" (Op. Cit. p. 70).

Individual psychology places the acting person at the center of everything. In his own words, "The human person is a conscious being, ordinarily aware of his reasons for his behavior"(Ibid). At this juncture, we are going to conclude this section by studying the 6 major concepts of Adler's Individual Psychology.

Among the 6 major concepts that are operative within Individual Psychology are:

Fictional finalism;

This refers to fictional goals or mental constructs of the hope personality because each person is motivated by hopes and aspirations, which may be achieved or not. But these hopes are there in the human hearts.

Striving for superiority;

This is the essence of "will to power". Every human person strives for excellence whether he achieves it or not, is not the case. But he must keep on trying till success is reached.

Inferiority feelings and compensation;

Because one fears failing one's exams, one has to work hard. In Adler's words, "The feelings of inferiority are the basis for all human improvements and creativity in the world" (Op. Cit. p. 72). As the popular saying goes, 'necessity is the mother of invention". But when these feelings of inferiority are exaggerated, it leads to mental illness or neurosis. When one faces life squarely with optimism, he strives for perfection, which is the ultimate goal of life.

Social interests;

That each person needs cooperation is important in any form of human personality development. The needs to develop social interest and feeling for others are the key in achieving one's goal in life. Selfish interest as implied in Freud's psychoanalysis is not welcomed in Adler's position. This movement to relate with others opens the doors for learning and socialization and happiness.

Style of life, and

The style of life one lives in adulthood is formed in early childhood and that to a great extent, determines his personality. For example, a friendly environment is likely to raise an individual who interacts amicably with others.

The 'creative self'

We have seen this earlier in the course of this discussion. This poses the question: "Who are you and of what stuff are you made of?" For Adler, "It is this creative self which gives a person meaning in life. It is the active principle of humanity. In essence, the doctrine of the 'creative self' asserts that man makes his own personality" (Op. Cit. p. 73). That is why in Adler's own words, he said: "It is a well-known fact that those who do not trust themselves will never trust others" (Alfred Adler, p. 145).

Finally, Adler has provided individuals with the tools they need to value their capacity to survive despite the uncertainties of life. Once they are aware of their will to power, they will stop at nothing to strive to excellence. Each person makes himself what he is. In a more practical manner, Adler's Individual Psychology fits well both in collectivist and individualistic cultures, including how ministers of the Gospel carry out their ministries, hence the next related issue on the moral implication of being a minister.

H. THE MORAL IMPLICATION OF BEING A MINISTER OF THE WORD OF GOD

In a book of this magnitude, one may begin to wonder why the issue of morality and ministers of the Gospel message is presented and discussed here. This is one of the challenging versions of the 21st Century educational systems, which GTF offers to the public and why psychology has to be valued in everyday life and interpersonal relationship. We still recapitulate that in chapter one of this book, the 'Background' precisely, we raised the following theological question, "What has psychology got to do with a religionist, Christian or traditionalist?" Studies have revealed that hypocrisy is self-deception and can lead to mental illness. We have equally noted it earlier that the life style one leads is determinant whether he or she lives or dies.

Therefore, the role morality plays in human life cannot be overemphasized, especially today when many people seem to deceive themselves with one religious claim or the other. This is to say, "The moral implication of being human" is a matter of great concern and cannot be dismissed with the wave of hand or can man be man and reasonably so, without morality? Besides, while we can have psychology without religion, the latter cannot exist without the former, which implies that religion, utilizes psychological tools for its operations. In this light, I have deemed it safer to discuss in the following order, those who morally claim to be religious leaders than the led:

1.   Who a minister is

2.   The general role of Ministers

3.   The target of the Word of God

4.   The meaning of morality and its implication in our context

We shall try as much as possible to be brief in each of these subjects. In a world such as ours, it has become so difficult to understand what is going on with God's words and His ministers because almost everybody is claiming to be one. Go to Nigeria for instance; the Church has become a lucrative business even here in America. We find such churches everywhere today, along the streets and market places. Worst still, many abandoned shops, mechanic workshops; shades have been converted to worshipping places. I am not against the worship of God or to mushroom churches all over. The problem is that most of these abandoned places are used for different odious activities in the name of the church. That is why the questions Nwachukwu has presented in his book, "Keeping Human Relationships Together" should be taken very seriously today. Read the book and discover yourself why an Atheist may be more acceptable to God than a hypocrite who occupies an elevated position in the church. Despite this, I am going to examine this topic according to the outline I have set up above. The first one I am going to examine concerns who these ministers are.

1. **Who a minister is:**

This is a context question that demands the same answer. It is contextual because, a minister in the government may be a minister in the church but with different life styles. Why? Our emphasis here is going to be centered on that of the church and how the minister can employ his rational faculties in dealing with human beings. In the 'FaithInTheWorkplace.com':

> *What comes to mind when you think of a minister? If you are like most people, you think about church and pulpits, preachers and priests, missionaries and Bible schoolteachers. And you would have good reasons to think of these people. They are acting in the office of diakonos. Throughout the epistles, this word is translated as minister. It is the source of our word 'deacon' (Marcus Goodyear, Internet source).*

The above expression limits a minister to the office of the deacon. Yet to be a deacon in American is not the same thing as being one in Nigeria. There is no married deacon in Nigeria but here we have some. According to Wikipedia:

> *In Christian churches, a minister is someone who is authorized by a church or religious organization to perform functions such as teaching of beliefs; leading service such as weddings, baptisms or funerals; or otherwise providing spiritual guidance to the community (Wikipedia, The Free Encyclopedia).*

In a sense, this definition is generally regarded as a minister in the church. In another instance, a minister can be called a 'pastor'. In the light of Wikipedia, "A pastor is an ordained leader of a Christian congregation" (Ibid). And the word 'pastor' comes from Latin meaning "shepherd". In the OT, shepherding refers to feeding of sheep. In the NT, the sheep refer to human beings. For instance, in Jeremiah, it is said, "Then I will give you shepherds after my own heart, who will feed you on knowledge and understanding" (Jeremiah: 3:15).

The knowledge and understanding mentioned above extend to psychology and how people can use it to advance the human conditions and enjoy better lives. In the NT, Jesus called himself the "Good Shepherd" (John 10:11), as recorded in John's Gospel. At another instance, Jesus told Peter to "shepherd my sheep" (John 21:16). No wonder, Paul said, "And he gave some as apostles, and some as prophets and some as evangelists, and some as pastors and teachers" (Ephesians 4:11). In a more drastic manner, Peter told the elders to "shepherd the flock of God among you" (1 Peter 5:1-2). From the foregoing discussions, it is easier for us to decipher the role of ministers based on their vocations as God's ambassadors on earth. The whole efforts ministers make are traceable to the value of psychology.

2. The general role of Ministers:

Our analyses above have pointed out the way we should go in this section – the general role of ministers. The various examples given above did not make allusion to the Sacraments of the Catholic Church, except in passing. However, we shall discuss in general terms what the roles of these ministers are in the world today, and the impacts those ministries have psychologically made on society and individual lives. In a nutshell, the general role of God's ministers is to bring the Gospel of peace, unity, reconciliation and love to society. The ministers are not called to become affluent or wealthy people in worldly standards. Unfortunately, most of the scandals witnessed today come from the ministers themselves. Do read Nwachukwu's "Self-assessment test – For ministers of the Gospel message" (Nwachukwu, 2010:184-188) and judge for yourself whether the ministers have actually carried out their roles as mandated by their Master or have ministered in their own names. When the aim of the Gospel is directed for selfish ends, psychology comes in to question the behaviors of such ministers.

3. The target of the word of God:

The target of the word of God is to teach people the way of the Lord and His principles, so that their actions and behaviors may be influenced by the same standards. In carrying out this fundamental mission, the ministers have to map out their plans and execute them in manners that will advance God's kingdom on earth, if not surface ministry becomes the end result and leaves society sicker than healthy. Jesus made it clear, "If anyone wishes to follow me, he must deny himself and take up his cross daily and follow me" (Luke 9:23). Taking up such a cross entails determination and governed by the hope that after all said and done, God will not abandon his people. Thus, psychology helps us to plan ahead and prefigure the consequences of our actions to avoid regrets. However, today every minister claims to be following the Lord, but some do not want to carry any cross let alone on daily basis. With the actions of some ministers of the Gospel today, the target of the word of God seems to have been misplaced by materialistic tendencies of some ministers. This misplacement of religious target is as the result of the lack of moral consciousness and how it can influence positive decisions and actions. When people feel positive to life, they enjoy better or good health and longevity.

4. The meaning of morality and its implication in our context

The issue of morality is deeply drummed in this book because bad life causes spiritual pains and leads to the sense of guilt too.

Most of our unconscious sicknesses are caused by remorse and they also lead to traumatic experiences. Good life or behavior is therapeutic. Psychological practice employs ethical values in an extensive capacity. For instance, a counselee who denies or hides the source of his or her problem (which might be immoral related or as a result of immoral behavior) may not receive the help he or she needs. Moral guilty creates problem in counseling. Morality in Nwachukwu's view is, "The quality in human acts by which we say they are right or wrong, good or evil" (Op.Cit, 2010:156). The only source through which these qualities are observed or known is by the way each person psychologically conducts him or herself in action. It has become evident to our senses that when we reflect on the prime target of God's words and the manners in which some ministers have maximized them for selfish interests, then, to read this book becomes very interesting – pointing to the moral implications of their ministries.

Today, society is in dire need of ministers by words and deeds. But most of the ministers are no longer after the salvation of souls but their personal aggrandizements and these attitudes complicate the focus of God's words and the actions of the ministers. Morality, being that quality of human actions through which society has come to realize what these ministers are doing, occupies a central place in psychological practice.

Morality, thus, cries out for divine assistance. While it is not good to blame all the ministers at a stretch, there are some of them that are creating confusion and misleading the public by their evangelism of monetary-siphoning-systems. Therefore, the moral implication of being a minister should be based on the good examples these ministers show to the general public by their actions. A minister is morally called to live up to his preaching and teaching. To preach one thing and do the opposite is morally not acceptable and hypocritical.

Let the ministers of God's words lead by good examples and not bad ones. Again, their failure to abide by what they teach is because most of them do not obey their consciences and lead by good examples. The need to be conscience-bound is important in psychological practice because psychology is man in his everyday life.

I. CONSCIENCE IS TO THE HUMAN HEART WHAT MORALITY IS TO LIFE

Our emphasis in this book is on life itself and how it can be lived reasonably. For this to happen, we have to employ psychology in its full meaning. We realize each other in action. In this book, therefore, both the heart and life are synonymous. Without the human heart, there is no life and there is life because the heart is alive too. The two must be preserved with uttermost care. One question that may stare us on the face is, "Is human life possible without conscience which serves as its ingredient?" Obviously, without any exaggerations, conscience is the essential aspect of human life. In this book therefore, it is my candid expectation to examine the factors that keep life moving or the heart healthy. Hence, the question that conscience is to the human heart what morality is to life itself? To address this issue scientifically, we need to understand the importance of psychology in the first place and the following three important items, the heart, conscience and morality in this order:

1. Conscience

2. The human heart and

3. Morality in comparison

Taking them one after the other, let us examine the meaning of conscience as to know what position it occupies in human heart as to psychologically influence human actions and behaviors.

1. **Conscience:**

According to Nwachukwu, "The engines of healthy relationships are within each individual" (Nwachukwu, 2010:214).We know what role an engine performs in the life of any machinery or car. In like manners, conscience is expected to perform the same role in human heart. No wonder, Nwachukwu further noted, "The power of the individual to care for and cure him or herself primarily comes from his or her positive memories, energized by sound moral life and good works and not from remorsefulness" (Ibid). This 'power' of the individual includes his power to live or die due to the style of life he has chosen. Hence, "conscience", according to Renard as quoted in Nwachukwu, means "An act by which we apply our knowledge of the moral principles in the practical intellect to what we do, did in the past or will do in future" (Op.Cit, 136). This is as interesting as the topic suggests. In Nwachukwu's interpretation of Renard, these unique human quality and facts, as stated above, are based on the premise that every human being has knowledge of these moral principles, which guide relationships. For instance, "any human being who is not guided by moral obligations and principles is more of a wild animal" (Ibid). The simple implication here is that once the human being ceases to behave as such, he is more of a dead object. In other words, his heart has stopped working.

2. **The human heart**

In ordinary human language, the heart is the center of life. When someone says, "I have given you my heart", it means that the person has totally devoted himself to the service of the other person, come rain, come sun. I remember in my hospital, when the code 1000 is sounded or given, it means there is a cardiac arrest, either, somebody has stopped to breathe or the heart has been affected. In medical perspective, we have so many types of heart, "The artificial, athletic, extra-corporeal heart etc" (The Free Dictionary by Farlex), all aimed at sustaining life. In another note, the Dictionary defines the heart as "the viscus of cardiac muscle that maintains the circulation of blood" (Ibid). Just as in the case of the engine oil of our cars, once there is none in them, the cars knock. The same thing happens in the case of the human heart, it has to pump blood to keep life on or moving, if not, one dies. Yet, the best ingredient of the heart is the feeling of joy one has in one's life.

The lack of internal peace and joy leads to emotional problems. The sense of joy or happiness does not come from evil deeds but good ones. According to one Internet source, "Happiness is an emotion that is characterized by a feeling of absolute contentment...a feeling of being where you should be" (Wikipedia, The Free Encyclopedia). In a more practical and implicating note, Wikipedia said, "Happiness is mediated through the release of so-called happiness hormones.... The happy person is a virtuous, meaning that they have outstanding abilities and emotional tendencies which allow him or her to fulfill our common human ends" (Ibid). This is where the importance of conscience has been noted and the major thing it does for the heart. A remorseful heart is almost as dead as the person who indulges in evil deeds.

3. Morality:

As noted earlier, psychology and morality are synonymous with rational beings. Based on what we have said already, can human life be possible without being morally good or positive? We had encountered this subject in our previous discussions that morality is the quality in human actions by which we say this action is good or evil. There is need to reiterate it for the purpose of the present discussion. Morality can best be understood in the context of conscience. For instance, in the language of Swani, cited in Nwachukwu, it says:

Conscience is light of the soul that burns within the chambers of your heart...voice of the self which says "yes" or "no" when you are involved in a moral struggle. It is a call from within to do an act or to avoid it. It is the internal monitor...a form of truth, which is the knowledge of our own acts and feelings as right or wrong. It is the sensitive balance (scales) to weigh actions. As a silent teacher, it is the soundless inner voice that shows you the path of virtue and godliness. It is above reason and discussion. It is sudden, dictatory command to plunge deep into the depths of virtue, or rise high above the levels of vice. It is a needle that points steadily to the Pole Star "Do this action, it is right" or "Avoid this action, it is wrong (Swani in Nwachukwu, 147-148).

From the foregoing examples, it is easy to see that conscience is interwoven with the heart, morality and life. They are inseparable. It has been emphasized here that conscience is the light of the soul, which burns within the chambers of our hearts. It is the voice which commands and urges us on to do or avoid a particular action, in order to enjoy the value of life itself. Conscience filters the human heart of all dirty feelings and fills it with energy, solace, peace and life. Conscience does its work silently without much noise.

As long as human beings listen to the teachings of virtue and morality, life progresses. It is a form of truth, which is psychologically the knowledge of our good actions. In other words, the role conscience plays in human heart by making it remain at ease without much worries from remorse of past bad deeds, morality does the same to life. In a sense, conscience is inseparable from morality because they play the same role. It is even easier to say that conscience is the foundation of morality. It reminds the agent of the implication of his actions. These are actions that could damage one's soul or heart and stagnate life itself.

Both the heart and morality have to align to function and keep the human person alive. In this sense, we see that the role conscience plays to alert the heart of those deeds that could damage it, morality does that to the whole person, showing him the best way to go as to live and avoid blames or death. We, as human beings need conscience to dictate for us the implications of our actions and morality to specify the way we must follow. It is only when our hearts are healthy because of the good lives we lead that life itself can psychologically have progress and peace and last. In this light, the need to differentiate or relate the meaning of morality to ethics is important here. Then, the next question springs up.

How does morality resemble ethics?

The above question is like asking the relationship that exists between parents and their children. This is why psychology is all about action and interaction. In the first place both parents and their children belong to human families. To have a child, there must be parents. In other words, parents come first before we can talk of their children. However, those we call children today will eventually become parents tomorrow if things follow their natural order. In the above question Nwachukwu posited, we see a similarity, "How does morality resemble ethics?" In this question, while we can regard ethics as the parent of the child, the child itself becomes morality in this comparison. Despite the comparison here, there is a little difference between the two issues involved. In the case of parent and child relationship, a child may become a parent tomorrow, without diminishing the position of its parents. On the other hand, ethics and morality can remain unchanged, without going through any metamorphosis. They do not undergo the changes found in parents and children relationships. With this in mind, we shall now begin to find out what the terms mean in our context.

1. Ethics:

Often we hear of one 'ethical principle or the other'. There is ethics in almost all walks of life, just like psychology, in the government, company, association, school system, medical profession as in nursing and medicine etc. The word "ethics" seems to be used to differentiate secular issues and to advance religious senses. Because this word is commonly used in everyday life or occurrences, it is important we find out its true meaning. Web definition holds it to mean, "Ethical motive, motivation based on ideas of right and wrong...the philosophical study of moral values and rules" (Website, Internet Resource). In another sense, "Ethics (also known as moral philosophy) is a branch of philosophy which seeks to address questions about morality; that is, about concepts such as good and bad, right and wrong, justice, and virtue" (Wikipedia, The Free Encyclopedia). According to the Church of Scientology, "Ethics may be defined as the actions an individual takes on himself to ensure his continued survival across the dynamics. Here, it becomes a personal thing. That is, when one is ethical, it is something "he does himself by his own choice" (Church of Scientology).

In Omar N. Bradley's own words, "Ethical – of or relating to philosophical study of ethics; 'ethical codes', 'ethical theories'... ethical – conforming to accepted standards of social or professional behavior; 'an ethical lawyer', ethical medical practice', 'an ethical problem'; 'had no ethical objection to drinking'. 'Ours is a world of nuclear giants and ethical infants'" (Omar N. Bradley – Internet Resource). Another source presents ethics as:

A system of moral principles. It is the rules or standards governing the conduct of a person or the members of a profession. It is a branch of philosophy concerned with the nature of ultimate value and the standards by which human actions can be judged right or wrong or simply 'Ethics is the philosophical study of values and rules (Internet Resources, 2011).

Definition of ethics by Voters, IR, holds, "Ethics is synonymous with morality; they mean the same thing. Morality is a belief about the difference between right and wrong. However, some people (like the German Philosopher Friedrich Nietzche) believe that there is no such thing as right and wrong because it all depends on your personal opinions. For instance, everyone in this country LOVES the UN, but I think UN has no place going around to places like China telling them what they can and can't do based on 'human rights" (Internet Resource).

On another shocking version, based on Friedrich's perspective regarding something that is right or wrong, "If someone believes that something is right, then they are lying because there will be, 100% of the time, other people telling them that they are wrong. There really is, in the scientific sense, no such thing as right or wrong, because there will always be someone who disagrees with you. No right, no wrong, only what you believe is right or wrong. If you believe that something is right, then it is right ...for you. That doesn't mean it is right, because it isn't wrong, either..." (Ibid).

The above views are obnoxious in the sense that morality cannot be based on personal whims and caprices. There are certain ethical principles that guide all rational beings. Let us examine the meaning of morality more closely before we can juxtapose the two terminologies – ethics and morality for a possible resemblance.

2. **Morality vis-à-vis ethics:**

Just as in the case of ethics, morality has close resemblance with it. In wordnetweb, morality, "Concerns with the distinction between good and evil or right and wrong, right or good conduct" (Friedrich Nietzche, Internet Resources).

In another sense, it states that, "Morality (from the Latin moralitas, 'manner, character, proper behavior') is a system of conduct and ethics that is virtuous. It can also be used in regard to sexual matters and chastity" (Wordnetweb.Princeton.edu/perl/webwn).

According to Standard Encyclopedia of Philosophy, "The term 'morality' can be used either;
Descriptively, to refer to a code of conduct put forward by

a. a society or,
b. some other group, such as a religion, or
c. accepted by an individual for her own behavior or

Normatively, to refer to a code of conduct that given specified conditions; would be put forward by all rational persons" (Wikipedia, The Free Encyclopedia).

However, many agree that, "Morality is an ambiguous term" (Standard Encyclopedia of Philosophy). For example, from its descriptive perspective or definition, "Morality is an unusual word. It is not used very much, at least not without qualification. People do sometimes talk about Christian morality, Nazi morality, or about morality of the Greeks, but they seldom talk simply about morality all by itself. Consistent with this way of talking, many anthropologists used to claim that morality, like law, applies only within a society. This view contradicts the views of those who base morality on personal decisions. They claim that morality refers to that code of conduct that is put forward by a society. However, even in small homogenous societies that have no written language distinctions are made among morality, etiquette, law, and religion" (Ibid).

At this point, I want to bring in Nwachukwu's view in order to examine how ethics and morality resemble each other. I believe, Nwachukwu's presentation on these terms throws more lights on the best thing to do. In his own view, "Ethics is particularly the science and study of morality" (Nwachukwu, 152) as noted earlier. On the other hand, "Morality is necessarily the basis for all human relationships" (Ibid). In Pope John Paul 11's view "Ethics is the science of human actions from the point of their moral value, of the good or evil contained in them. Every human action involves a particular lived experience that goes by the name ethical experience.... This whole lived experience has a thoroughly, empirical character" (Wojtyla's Lectures, 1993: 23).

From Nwachukwu's observation so far on this issue, it is easy to understand that ethics and morality have real resemblances. Again, we saw in our previous papers that morality is that quality in human actions by which we think positively, do things right and enjoy good health or negatively and suffer on account of our evil behaviors and bad choices, while ethics is the study of those qualities that boost our ego integrity. The issue is made very clear here. As noted previously, values of good choices and behaviors have healing effects in themselves

However, I do vehemently disagree with those systems that hold that ethics or morality depends on one's choices. Ethics is not a personal thing. While I agree on the relativism of ethics and morality because of cultural diversities and differences, yet there are certain actions that are conventionally accepted as belonging to human beings and whose violations are evil thereof. For instance, murder or stealing is ethically evil and must be avoided at all times irrespective of the individuals and cultures involved in it. Yet, many rational beings behave like brutes. As such, we have to investigate if these brutes or animals are morally bound in their actions as to determine why some human problems defile diagnoses.

J. TO WHAT EXTENT ARE BRUTE ANIMALS MORALLY BOUND?

This is one of the toughest questions Prof. Nwachukwu presented in his e-tutorial lectures, which I have adopted and incorporated in this book. In the light of our discussion, does psychology apply to animals? This is where the value of psychology is so extensive, because it applies to every created living thing, trees, humans, vegetation, brutes and what have you. As humans, we are all familiar with our relationships with brute animals. I know that human beings are equally animals but not on the same degrees and levels with brute ones. But to ask whether these animals are morally bound is not as easy as it sounds.

In real life situations, we have seen many animals behave like human beings in terms of errands and messages. For example, some dogs run errands for their owners, defend and save them in face of danger. Even in some cases, it has been published on International news, National Geographic Channels, and some other media how dogs helped to save the lives of their owners. Camels carry loads for their owners too. When we watch the animal kingdoms, we discover that monkeys do funny things as humans. What of dolphins that play with humans as equals in some occasions? Police dogs are even trained as detectives. They perform actions most humans cannot at times.

In all these, can we say that animals are culpable for their wrong actions? Actually, we blame our dogs when they behave badly. But the question is, "Are they conscious of the moral implications of their actions or behaviors?" This is the core of the question. To what extent are they blamable for their wrong doings? We need some clues to draw our conclusions here since all living things exercise one form of psychology in their behaviors or the other. To place human beings where they belong as different from other animals, we shall examine some clues, which are psychologically oriented.

a. First Clue:

In Nwachukwu's writing, "Generally, there should be a consensus of opinions regarding certain behaviors and mannerisms that identify, define and characterize a human society as different from those of other animals" (Nwachukwu, 2010:137). In other words, despite the fact that we share certain qualities with animals like in the case of reproduction, sense of perceptions, sensory senses – "smell, hear, taste and touch" (Op.Cit, 249), there is still a difference. Nwachukwu made a serious demarcation here, "There is a difference between 'actus humanus' – human act and 'actus humanis' – an act of man, typical of brutes" (Op.Cit, 137). These differentiations are important in this writing. Human acts pertain to humans as rational beings while an act of man refers to animals as brutes. It does not matter the level of trainings animals have been given today to perform certain actions that look rational like those of humans, I still do not agree that they are morally bound for those actions. According to Doug McManaman's story, our point of argument becomes clearer, "Recently I heard a story of a man who suffered a heart attack while walking his dog. The dog would not allow paramedics near the man to treat him, and so police had to be called in to shoot the creature. The delay resulted in the man's death" (Doug McManaman, Internet Resource). Though, the dog actually acted in defense of his master, because it had no reasoning ability, its action resulted to its own death and that of its master.

b. Second Clue:

We are going to move forward from the above story. Indeed, brute animals are marvelous and wonderful creatures. But from the story just told, as noted above, if the dog knew what was happening, it could have allowed the life of his owner to be saved. But it did not. In line with the Internet Resource, "A categorical proposition is a complete sentence with a subject and a predicate. For example: "Giraffes are tall". "Giraffe" is the subject, and "tall" is the predicate. The genus in a definition is that which is predicated essentially of several things that differ in species. For example, a bird is an animal, a dog is an animal, a horse is an animal, and a man is an animal. As we can see, "animal" is predicated of bird, dog, horse, and man.

Furthermore, "animal" is predicated essentially of them all, not non-essentially" (Ibid). In a more powerful instance, man is not defined along with animals because of their colors or certain biological features. Doug reacting to this factor maintained, "One cannot predicate "brown" essentially of bird, dog, horse, and man, even though all of them might be brown. The color brown is not part of the very essence of man; otherwise all men would be brown. Nor is brown part of the very idea of bird, otherwise all birds would be brown, and anything that isn't brown, like a Blue jay or a Cardinal, would not be a bird. But animal is part of the essence of man, bird, horse, and dog. If a thing is not an animal it cannot be a dog" (Doug McManaman, IR), or found in that family. Syllogistically, dog is an animal.

c. Third Clue:

It has become important to state categorically clear that all animals are not the same. We are all mammals – warm-blooded animals but not of the same essence and identity. While we do not deny that animals are intelligent, the cognitive ability to reason and make calculations belongs to the human kingdom. Even though animals could be trained to perform professional actions like the police dogs, they cannot go beyond the training given to them because they do not have analytic minds and reasons. We share many qualities in common as already noted, in terms of physicals, but not on the level of reasoning or intellectuals.

According to these elaborate website evaluations here:

Now, the specific difference is that which reduces the genus to a species, making one species essentially different from another within a genus. Hence, "sentient" is the specific difference that renders an animal essentially different from a rose. Man is a living sentient creature as well, but "animal" is the genus in the definition of man, and the definition is that which expresses what a thing is essentially. What is it that reduces the genus "animal" to the species "man"? The answer to that question is none other than the ability to reason. Man is a rational animal. To be rational is to have the ability to draw a necessary conclusion from given premises (Internet Resources).

In other words, despite the fact that man and brute animals belong to the same genus or group, and are all sentient, having the ability to perceive things, there is still an ocean of difference. It is absurd to group or count man within the same class with other animals because they share certain similarities. If it is possible to do that, what then prevents man claiming to be God since he is created in God's image of holiness and purity?

d. Fourth Clue:

Life is larger than logic. In drawing conclusions, one has got to be very careful. For instance, to say that some students failed because they have not worked hard does not follow in all circumstances. According to website resources:

In order to reason, one must be able to make judgments, for example, "Some things are not men" or "All men are animals". The ability to make universal statements (all men are animals), however, presupposes the ability to apprehend universal concepts, such as "man", "animal", "thing", "living", "health", "equality", "universality", "cause", "science", "essential", "necessity", "contingency", etc (Internet Resource).

From the above syllogism, it is possible that a student who worked hard through the course of his or her programs may fail due to a lot of reasons, sickness, teacher's manipulations, loss of original transcripts or papers etc. Again, universal concepts are not as sensible as particulars which are. In the sensible level, we speak of what we can perceive, touch, or communicate with. In other words, for us to ascertain whether animals are moral or not, we need to objectify our claims and base our comparison here. We cannot just draw a picture of the concept of anything; say man or animal without any qualifications and objectivity. In our present comparison, when we talk of man, a lot go with it. Just as in the case of animal. When we speak of animals, what animals actually are we talking about here, a goat, a fowl, a horse, a dog, a cow, a bird? Does the word "animal" cover all of them or exclude any? That is why the Internet resource we consulted here insists:

'Animal' is not necessarily four legged, or two legged, or winged or not winged. It has no corresponding image. It is an idea, that is, something intelligible, not sensible. Nor can we draw a picture of the idea or species "bird" a priori without any evidence-based figure. One can only illustrate an image, that is, a particular bird of a particular species (i.e., canary, duck, falcon, etc.), having a particular size, color, etc. But universal concepts have no size, shape, color, or texture. What color is the idea or concept "color"? It is neither red nor green nor blue. How long is the concept of length? How small is the idea of small? To what is the idea of "relation" related?

What shape is the concept "shape"? Is it round, square, or rectangular? (Ibid).

According to the law of quantum physics, an observer cannot be separated from the observation he or she is making. It is one thing to say that animals have brains or intelligent, but another to say to what extent their brains or intelligence can be compared with those of human beings. This is the mistake most people make. For the simple fact that some dogs perform heroic acts does not make them equal to man or culpable for certain actions. It is precisely why this source, in an extensive passage, observes:

All of us know what it means to be small, heavy, colored, one, many, true, false, good, beautiful, honest, healthy, and sick, etc. But none of these are sensible. Universal ideas have no sensible matter, and what is material cannot be the receiving subject of what is immaterial. The hand cannot grab a concept as it can grab a hammer, and the eye cannot behold the concept "health", "equation", or "necessity". We cannot taste "quantity", or morality", or the very concept "taste". The receiving subject must be proportioned to what it receives, which is why the mind and the brain are not the same thing. The brain is the organ of internal sensation (sense memory, imagination, instinct, kinesthetic sensation, etc), and sensation is always of particulars (Ibid).

As a matter of comparison, can we say that animals share the above attributes and qualities on equal capacity with man? While we do not doubt that animals have brains, predicating the faculty of imagination to animals is the same thing as saying that they are involved in abstract thinking like humans. Whether we like it or not, the human mind is an immaterial power or faculty in whose object is mainly the intelligible structure of things. In other words, the nature of things as we know them and how an idea exists in our minds, are within the realm of universal. In this instance, it is necessary to borrow from the same Internet Source which holds:

> *Animals have brains, because they are sentient creatures, but they don't have minds. Whenever I want my own dog out of the house, all I do is open the side door and call out "squirrel", and she will run out and into the backyard barking and searching all around for it every time, for the past 7 years in fact. The reason is that in her sense memory, the sound "squirrel" is associated with the phantasm of a squirrel as a result of past experience with us, and that phantasm evokes an instinctive reaction. She does not understand the concept of falsehood or deception, whereas children do. That is why one can fool a child once or twice, but not indefinitely" (Website view Resources).*

Even though some animals know those who hate them, but they can easily be deceived than human beings, even babies. Thus, animals are not morally bound for their actions, period. Hence, the need to preserve life through bioethical studies today is essential. The ability to understand the qualities that characterize and define us as human beings, the better for us to fully appreciate why some of us suffer from emotional problems. Life is so precious, anything that can be done to preserve it, is on the right side of God's law.

K. BIOETHICS - THE APPLICATION OF NATURAL SCIENCES TO MODERN MEDICINE: RELATATIONSHIP WITH RELIGION AND MORALITY

This is very interesting because of the emphasis on life today. A lot of studies have been carried out on this area of bio-ethics that deals directly with life. No wonder the connection with medicine is important. In this book however, I am going to discuss the importance of bio-ethics and its relevance in medicine, underlying the value of psychology therein. At the same time, there is need to understand its relationships with religion and morality and how they differ too. In my previous discussions on religion and morality, I dealt extensively with these terms and how they impact human life in general and that of an individual in particular. Practically, we cannot discuss the relevance of bioethics without mentioning morality. Thus, I am going to follow some orders to address these concerns. These orders will include:

1. The term, "bioethics"
2. Relevance in medicine
3. Differences in bioethics, [if any], and relationship with morality and religion

By the time we have examined the implications of the above issues, the thrust of this book would have scored a higher percentage, especially in the areas of psychological practice. The prime target of the book is to assist people to build some internal energy and muscles to squarely deal and face their problems.

1. **The term, "bioethics"**

People have held different opinions about this matter in different ways. According to a website definition: "It is the branch of ethics that studies moral values in the biomedical sciences" (Wordnetweb. princeton.edu/perl/webwn). It is interesting to note from the definition that bioethics is part of ethics. This means, without ethics we should not have had anything like bioethics. In another version, "Bioethics is the philosophical study of the ethical controversies brought about by advances in biology and medicine. Bio-ethicists are concerned with the ethical questions that arise in the relationships among life sciences, biotechnology, medicine, politics, law, philosophy, and theology" (en.wikipedia.org/wkik/Bioethics).

In the above presentations, few factors are implicated namely; scientific study of ethics, ethical controversies, discoveries of modern science on life. Practically, bioethics is aiming at finding out the applications of ethical principles in medicine. The controversies talked about here concern certain life decisions, as whether to protect it or not, and the researches that are being carried out today without any reference to moral and religious implications. Eventually, these controversies are brought about by the discoveries of modern sciences on life issues.

In this line of argument, another source holds that bioethics is, "The study of ethical issues raised by research on living beings and the applications of that research" (www.temasactuales.com/tools/glossary2.php), on those living beings. In effect, this latest definition is simple to understand and analyze. Bioethics is the study of ethical matters or issues brought about by discoveries or research on living things, including animals and humans and how these findings could be applied to the subject of this study – life. As I said, based on this definition, we can go ahead to discuss the relevance of the study itself.

2. Relevance in medicine

Before I can justify this section in this book, I will like to explain in a nutshell what medicine stands for, in our context. In the first place, the basic question that should concern us here is, "What does it mean to be alive?" (Arthur Caplan, IR). Arthur has wondered at scientific movements and how "scientists alter genes to create living bacteria from non-living parts" (Ibid). We need to answer this fundamental question before we can begin to argue whether bioethics should be based on medical or ethical principles of preservation of life itself. Arthur Caplan, reacting to the above question, observes, "That's a weighty question that scientists, theologians and philosophers have been wrangling over for eons. Most have concluded that the wondrous nature of what permits life is a mystery that science never could penetrate" (Ibid). I equally agree with Arthur that no scientific investigations could contradict the basis of life itself as a mystery. It is one thing to study life and another for life to be what it is, inviolable, irrespective of all scientific investigations and enquiries.

At this point, it is necessary to understand the meaning of medicine in our context. According to an Internet source, medicine means either of the following:

> *The branches of medical science that deal with non-surgical techniques; something that treats or prevents or alleviates the symptoms of disease; the learned profession that is mastered by graduates training in a medical school and that is devoted to preventing or alleviating or curing diseases and injuries (wordnetweb.Princeton.edu/perl/webwn).*

The manner in which we approach others in their problems can also be medicinal. The above explanation presupposes the preservation of life. In other words, both medicine and bioethics are concerned with life, the emphasis may be different.

Again, from the above definition, it is obvious that medicine is aimed at restoring the good health of somebody who is sick and the factors that might affect this fundamental foundation - life. This is also the focus of bioethics, the study of ethical values and their applications on the protection of life. There are both traditional medicines in which family members, friends and such friendly-related associations are involved. In Africa, extended family system plays major and therapeutic roles here. The modern medicine, on the other hand, focuses on scientific appliances, diagnoses and administrations of drugs to cure sickness or diseases, while the counseling psychology employs skills and techniques to bring healing to the afflicted.

3. **Differences in bioethics**, [if any], and relationship with morality
   and religion

There is no doubt that "Bioethics is primarily the application of psychology or natural sciences to modern medicine. How it relates to or differs from religion and morality is a different question. The comparison is realized in many ways. By natural sciences here we mean all the modern scientific approaches in handling human sicknesses. Natural sciences study the physical phenomena of this world and how the affect life in general, including the lives of other animals. Biological studies are some of the aspects of natural sciences. In our context, these sciences form the basis for understanding human physiological components and the best ways to understand them, whether in good health or sickness.

Thus, bioethics, which is the ethics of life, becomes an important tool for addressing life from different perspectives, morally, theologically, religiously, medically, philosophically etc. In each of these spectra, life is at the center. The relationship we are talking about comes from the way modern science looks at life from these perspectives already mentioned, especially in morality and religion. Any scientific study that contradicts human life, liberty and pursuit of happiness is considered immoral, and most often religion frowns at such studies or findings. From the religious points of view, life is unique and precious and anything that goes against it, either from medicine, science or technology is not acceptable.

In this context, there is a big connection between bioethics, morality and religion. The only difference comes from the cultural diversities that are pertinent in society today. While certain cultures might accept traditional medicine as the best ways to cure sickness, the western world prefers modern medicine. In this sense, we find that certain treatments are acceptable in some areas but shunned others.

Again, religion is never consulted in the application of modern medicine to people. This is a big difference. But the impact modern medicine makes on people might provoke religious reactions and approval. Hence, bioethics has to be encouraged from the points of view of making efforts to preserve human lives and those of other animals. In all these comparisons, morality plays a major role also. In order for the counselor to be morally fit and be more effective, especially today that there are cases of abuses and scandals, there is need to know if being religious is the same thing as being moral.

L. BEING MORAL VIS-À-VIS BEING RELIGIOUS

In an issue like this, psychology is at the foundation of both religion and morality. The question was almost framed in the same way as the one I handled in spirituality and psychology. Thus, "Is being spiritual the same as being religious?" The difference here is the fact that morality takes the place of 'spiritual' and the two are not exactly the same thing but can cut across each other. In a way, I am going to recapitulate some of my earlier arguments in this presentation, but within the present heading. As we read Nwachukwu's work on Spiritual Psychology, we discover that he is consistent in maintaining a convincing argument regarding religion and morality. Here again, we are presented with another challenging question as regards whether morality is the same thing as religion. As I have always said, I have benefited richly from the academic systems at Graduate Theological Foundation. In many instances, people mean religion when they speak of morality and verse versa. That is why, in complementing someone as being religious, it includes his or her morality and spirituality as well. This is because most of the people who claim to be spiritual and religious equally presume that they are inclusively moral.

As a scientific enquiry, we are not going to make any conclusion till we have studied and examined the terminologies employed therein. The question, "To be moral is to be religious" can create a problem for people who are not versed in scientific studies as the one being discussed here. As I have always maintained, this is my joy and strength for this opportunity to study a course that assists me understand and appreciate the concerns of other people. As it holds, let me first of all present these terms in manners that can assist us make the impending comparison, as it connects morality and religion.

We have said it already that the word "Morality" is foundational to human interrelatedness, employed in its descriptive and normative perspectives. From our previous studies in these subjects, their importance and needs in human situations have been highlighted. By morality being descriptive, it describes a situation, a principle, a code of conduct that a particular society has put in place that has to guide her actions and behaviors. As noted above, morality is equally used to refer to religious functions. It is true when we consider different religious groups who emphasize particular mannerism or attitudes whose compliance is not optional. But can we say that these attitudes mean morality in essence? We are yet to understand that. The above Web definition equally alludes to the fact that morality is a code of conduct, which an individual has imposed upon himself for the guidance of his or her actions. In this manner, the source already noted did not tell us whether this imposition is done to avoid being punished or for religious reasons or just for one to be good in life.

Again, morality serves as a form of normative, a type of law specifying a general conformity, whose derailment results to punishment. It does not matter what step we take here, for Nwachukwu, "Morality is that quality in human action by which we say it is good or bad, right or wrong" (Nwachukwu, 156). In this sense, we do not regard it as descriptive or normative. Rather it applies to human beings as distinct from all other animals. There is a way of characterizing human actions. If there is no difference in what human beings do, whether good or bad, can we still claim to have reasons or rationality? This is the central message. In other words, are all human actions religious and moral at the same time? We need to recapitulate our knowledge of religion for us to understand the matter properly.

Meaning of Religion:

The word "Religion" is commonly used today to refer to those who worship God. At times, religious people are seen as groups who have dedicated themselves to carry out one belief or the other. In the practice of religion, psychology has to be employed also. Just as we say that "morality is an ambiguous term" (Standard Encyclopedia of Philosophy), so is religion. Some religious groups may not have anything to do with the Christian group just as some may not even practice religion in the real sense of it. Most people have used religion as an undercover identity to perpetuate evil in the world today. Different secret societies use religion to carry out their nefarious and heinous deeds. In a more pronounced manner, religion has been a private thing for those who nurse one belief system or the other. No wonder most governments of the world have stripped religion off the school curriculum, mainly to avoid strives and conflicting religious atmosphere. People can practice what they believe in and those who do not have one, will not be treated less in the government or society, hence the emphasis on religious freedom.

On the basis of our discussion here, different people who employ it for one reason or the other have psychologically defined religion differently. As a Catholic from birth, religion means much to me. Yet I see some of our nurses who believe in nothing jeer at me when I hold my Rosary during free or break time. A lot of them have asked me what the Rosary means. Based on my wealth of experiences and belief in what I do as Catholic, I cannot understand how a human being can be happy without religion or a belief in a higher power that supervises the physical world. Yet my worries do not seem to bother some of my colleagues and some of them who claim to have religion do not show any sign that it means anything in their lives.

No wonder, Gordon quoted in Nwachukwu remarked, "There are two kinds of religion: Instrumental – which serves God for what you can get out of it; and the Intrinsic religion – which serves God regardless of what the consequences of that might be" (Gordon in Nwachukwu, page 166).

In the light of what individuals fight to gain in religion, psychology is the key. Based on my conviction as reflected earlier in this book, closer look at the above definition or expression Gordon made here has a striking revelation. Today, it appears that this instrumental dimension of religion is the order of the day in society and world around. Most of those who claim to have religion or worship God seem to be hypocritically oriented. In this instance can we say that these people are morally good or bad? We are talking of actions that have already taken place. As Nwachukwu put it, "For an act to be morally evil means it has already been performed" (Op.Cit, 241).

Eventually, our emphasis here presupposes those behaviors and actions whose consequences have already affected and influenced the human society. Nwachukwu once noted in his book that the devil does not know what we have in mind till we act or say something which he uses later on to fight us. Practically, "a moral act is an act which is performed with knowledge and freedom" (Murray in Nwachukwu, 258). In every moral action, psychology is freely and consciously or unconsciously employed in the decision-making.

Therefore, at this point, it is easy to ask ourselves, is being moral the same thing as being religious? Judging from what has preceded this conclusion, there is something we must understand. When a person indulges in religious hypocrisy and deceit, is his action morally sound or evil? The force of religion and morality should be based on action. If an action is bad, it is morally so, but if it is good, it is morally good. In this way, it does not matter whether a believer performs that act or not. What matters is the effect of the action on others. The relativism of morality should not constitute any obstacle here. One culture's meat could be another's poison. Yet there are certain actions that should be conventionally and universally accepted as normative in nature, whereby what obtains in America can equally obtain in Africa or in all parts of the globe as I noted before. For instance, we owe it to one another to tell others the truth, love and treat them with kindness irrespective of their level of reciprocity.

When someone who believes in God continually tells lies or behaves in an unacceptable or evil manner, even if his actions appear innocent in the eyes of the world, he or she should be taken as morally evil. Yet, in any act of deceit or righteousness, psychology is at the center. In this way, it is easy to say that to be moral is not the same thing as being religious because the human mind is deeply packed with untested ideas and fantasies. Yet in certain instances, to be moral can be justified as being religious when the person who is religious takes into account and considers the effects of his actions on other people. It is not enough for anybody to claim that he is moral and religious when he goes around deceiving others.

One is morally good or not, depending on what one does and so is the person who has religion. Using religion to dupe people is not the essence of religion, but an attitude that is universally condemned as moral evil. We can now understand why a lot of people are suffering from emotional problems. We all need emotional intelligence or 'intellectual virtue' according to Nwachukwu, in order to visualize ahead of time, the consequences of what we do now, did yesterday and intend to do in future.

There are people whose health situation has nothing to do with the administration of drugs or medication but purely therapeutic. Why? In as much as we shall not continue to repeat the points we have made previously in this book, it is important to note that bad life style is the number one cause and killer of human progress, success and lives. We enter into psychological problems, especially when we think we have all it takes to live in our world without any reference to neighbors and God.

M. THEOLOGICAL PERSPECTIVES OF THE NEED FOR PSYCHOLOGY

A. The Old Testament:

In the first place, there is need to note that the Old Testament has much to say about physical and psychological suffering. The evidences are not far-fetched as we can infer from different kinds of personal suffering and experiences. Suffering is part and parcel of human life, theologically as a result of sin. For instance, when God drove away or expelled Adam from the Garden of Eden, he informed him of the impending danger that was to come, "Because you listened to your wife and ate from the tree of which I had forbidden you to eat" (Genesis 3:17), you are going to face the music. Biblically, it was the beginning of the history and origin of human suffering. Due principally to that initial disobedience to God, the human race, ipso facto, made God's blessed land to become a curse and punishable. That curse was 'suffering and death', which has perpetuated throughout mankind.

Eventually, the consequent effects were the expulsion of Adam and Eve from the garden. The Book of Genesis informs us of how and why suffering became an integral part of human experience. According to the Psalmist, suffering leads to repentance and an acknowledgment of faults; it prompts us to conversion (Psalm 32:4-5). The sufferings of those I have encountered in my life journey compelled me into this mission or compassionate undertaking.

In similar way, it makes God to forgive us our transgressions. For instance, when God heard the boy wailing, the angel of the Lord enquired, "What is the matter, Hagar? Don't be afraid; God has heard the boy's cry in this plight of his" (Genesis 21:17). In Exodus, "The Israelites groaned and cried out because of their slavery. As their cry for release went up to God, he heard their groaning and was mindful of his covenant" (Exodus 2:23-24). Today, we are all called in similar manner to be our brother's keepers. In Exodus 3:7, 2 Kings 20:5, God was also moved to compassion and forgiveness. Suffering brings reward from God (Genesis 22:16), especially when the sufferer is patient and hopeful.

The popular story of Noah revealed how God used suffering to start a new world (Genesis 6:1-9:17). If God had wished to extinct humanity from the face of their sins, none of us could have been alive today. After God saw how wickedness had formed part of man's culture, as it is today, how people had become bad, he went ahead to rescue us. In a way, humanity had not only disobeyed God, but also gone into atrocious pattern of life styles. That was the main reason why God wanted to destroy his creation. The violation of the created order led humanity into a mess and God decided to wipe away the whole human race from the face of the earth with flood.

The same suffering reached its zenith in the book of Job. The book of Job demonstrates an example of a painful personal and unique experience of sufferer and suffering of an innocent person. Yet, in the midst of suffering, Job remained faithful to his God. What an example for humanity to learn? His action was a very big and great lesson for us all, as cited in his response, "But as for me, I know that my Vindicator lives, and that he will at last stand forth upon the dust" (Job 19:25). The example should be therapeutic for people in similar situations. Thus, we should always hope for salvation in the midst of our sufferings.

On another practical example, Jeremiah was one of the most worthy men that lived, but he turned out to become the prophet of woes due to his personal experiences. He was so distressed that he wished that it had been good that he was not born. In other words, he cursed the womb that bore him (Jeremiah 15:15 -18). He felt so lonely, discouraged, depressed and bitter to a point that he even accused God, expressed his bitterness and felt no peace, joy or happiness for being called to ministry. No wonder today, he was identified and known as a weeping prophet (Lamentation 3:48).

The Old Testament tries to console us in our sufferings and that God knows and cares more than we go through in our sufferings. The OT conceives suffering in a general sense and used it to refer to our physical and moral evil and encourages us to bear our suffering patiently so that suffering can be redeemed. It was in this line of thought that Van Der Poel wrote this long passage,

> *Suffering shakes a person out of his or her self-confidence, opens the individual to the process of healing, and leads to recognition of God's presence and authority. In Exodus 15:26 – God asks people to listen to his commands. He warns then that he is the master of life and death (Deut 32:39). God both gives punishment and healing (Is 19:22, 30:26; Hosea 6:1, Jeremiah 31:19). Suffering is a form of chastisement, it purifies*

devotion to God, and it helps in the process of healing. God's mercy is not absent. Jeremiah (10:24) prays to God...., Confer Lam. 3:32-33, Ps. 30, 31. Suffering leads to repentance and acknowledgment of faults; it becomes a prompt to conversion (Ps. 32:4-5, 34:19, 51:19). Suffering moves God to compassion and forgiveness (Gen. 21:17, Ex. 2:24, 3:7, 2 kings 20:5, Tobit 3:16). Suffering brings reward from God (Gen 22:16, 1 Sam 2, 2 Macchabees 7:11.) Suffering is a source of atonement (cf. Comelius Van der Poel, "Wholeness and Holiness...1999: 80).

By the above elaborate passage, in all situations in life, we should have hope. The God we serve is an awesome God, ever faithful to show that his love and his mercy never end. God allows his chosen nation to suffer in other to open a way to show His mighty protection, because he could write on crooked lines.

Other powerful Messengers of God included Moses and Elijah. From the Bible, we saw how both of them wanted to die due to their bad situations. The chastisements of God are demonstrated in the biblical passages:

a. The flood in Genesis 6;

b. The story of Sodom and Gomorrah, Genesis 19;

c. The 10 plagues in Exodus 7-12 all show.

From these stories of suffering in the Old Testament, we understand the reality of suffering and the experiences of suffering, which are beyond human control. Thus, people can only search for the meaning, and will continue to search for its meaning rather than its source.

The unavoidability of suffering has to be noted too. Whether we accept it or not, suffering is unavoidable. When we accept suffering in patience; it becomes a source of forgiveness and renewed friendship with God who gives us protection on daily basis. The effect of suffering as laid down in the Old Testament and carried over into the New Testament has much to teach us. There is an important link, which the Bible provides between the Old Testament's sacrificial system and the New Testament's new dispensation or convention that Jesus Christ's death atones for sin. Jesus said on the cross, it is finished and that is the joy of all Christians and humanity that believes in him. Even though we have to face our suffering in faith, it leads us to the understanding that suffering is realized in the context of the New Testament.

B. The New Testament:

The New Testament begins with the incarnation of Jesus Christ, called the new dispensation. It is filled with some significant and important passages concerning suffering. The massacre of the innocent children as ordered by Pharaoh seemed to have begun the recording of suffering in the NT. Most of the experiences of suffering in the New Testament are epitomized and centered on the sufferings of Christ, which gives meaning to the sufferings of his disciples and of humanity in general, especially his followers. While Jesus came to deliver us from sin, he went about it through the most excruciating process of suffering and made it clear to his disciples that they would expect the same thing - suffering. We read the timely warning he gave them in Mark and Matthew's Gospels, (Mark. 8:35, Matthew 10:38).

In another fashion, he said, "Whoever wishes to come after me must deny himself, take up his cross, and follow me" (Mark 8:34). To take up a cross is not like eating and drinking. It entails pain. We suffer not because of our own sins alone, but the sins of our brothers and sisters. He, Jesus explained it that an individual's suffering is not correlated to his personal sins (Luke 13:1-5) and that the devil equally causes suffering (Rev. 2:9-10). In a practical manner, he stated that not all our sufferings are as the results of sin (John 9:1-3). He predisposed us to face the daily challenges with optimism.

The notion of suffering in the New Testament was centered on the suffering of Jesus, starting from his earthly life and most importantly ending up with his crucifixion and death on the cross. Jesus showed us a perfect example of what it meant to suffer. His suffering was not only physical but also psychological. He was humiliated, spat upon, beaten up, jeered at, nailed on the cross and left to die miserably in anguish with name calling, nasty remarks and comments.

Consequently, in the same way, our everyday sorrow and pain should be our crosses for our salvation and for the sake of Jesus (Philippians 1:29). We should see suffering as a participation in the salvific role of Christ, especially for us Christians. The statement of St. Paul to the Colossians should be very encouraging as we read, "Now I rejoice in my suffering for your sake, and in my flesh I am filling up what is lacking in the afflictions of Christ on behalf of his body, which is the church" (Colossians 1:24). Thus, we are all called to bear some sufferings for the sake of our brothers and sisters too.

We already quoted Van Der Poel's notion of suffering in this work. Thus;

> *Suffering and healing are essential perspectives in the life and teaching of Jesus as well as in the life and teaching of his followers. It is particularly the redemptive element of suffering that is of the highest importance (Van Der Poel, 1999:79).*

When we suffer for others' sins, our sufferings become redemptive. It was the point St. Peter noted in his first letter. He made it clear that we would suffer for our own sins, and also suffer as a result of doing well (1Peter 2:20; 3:17). Definitely, suffering or sickness takes somebody to a different country and that is why suffering speaks the language, which only the sufferer understands better. No wonder Van Der Pole reiterated, as observed above that, "Suffering shakes a person out of his or her self-confidence, opens the individual to the process of healing, and leads to recognition of God's presence and authority (Van der Poel, 1999:80).

The story of the Prodigal son invites each of us to return home from our long journey of sufferings, lives of indiscipline and sins. The Bible beautifully summarized it in this way, "When he had freely spent everything, a severe famine struck that country, and he found himself in dire need" (Luke 15:14-18). God warns us on daily basis to return home and embrace our loving father who is always waiting to welcome us from our sins. Once we conquer our suffering through our hope in God, we feel invigorated and happy. God loves sinners but hates their sins.

Eventually, we should know that suffering is a problem in life that comes to everyone without any exceptions. Both the Old and the New Testaments have testified to the power our God has, to conquer suffering in order to manifest his glory. But being impatient can lead us to more psychological sufferings. By suffering, we build our character and face our daily challenges squarely.

Suffering can be a test for our spiritual maturity, leading us to perseverance and confidence to survive. St. Paul instructed that by suffering, we improve our character and that improved character can produce hope – what kind of hope - a spiritual hope (Romans 5:1-2). As such, if we share in Jesus' sufferings on earth, then we will share in His glory in heaven (Romans 8:17-18) because the heavenly examinations have already taken place on earth.

At this point in our enquiry, it becomes important to examine the methodology through which this undertaking was designed, planned and developed. The book was a child of research and great concern for people going through one devastating experience in their lives or the other.

CHAPTER THREE

A CASE STUDY

(With a Patient with emotional frustration due to Spinal Dislocation)

The Demographic Study

Research methodology is all about how far the researcher came to a particular conclusion, area of investigation or developed the thesis, monograph or the book at hand. In the first place, I am constrained to note that this very book is a continuation of the concern I have always sought both in the nursing profession in order to provide a panacea to the sick at the hospital where I work. However, in the present compensation, my concentration is shifted to the need for psychology in everyday life, including the area of religious practices.

Thus, I chose to employ the same demographic approach I had in my nursing profession to develop this deep concern I have for people in various emotional situations. Feelings have no banks of their own, and the effort each person makes to respond to a particular emotional need, goes a long way to bring supportive presence to each other. Listening ability can also solve problems which no money on earth can, hence, the urgency and relevance of this book.

Therefore, by posing and presenting the fundamental need of psychological practice in society at this time is ad rem and classic. As already drummed repeatedly in this book, the need for human beings to be conscious of what they do and the consequences thereupon are important tools in psychological practice. Life is an on-going process governed by elements of change, and psychology is the only vehicle through which these elements of change are monitored and directed. This is precisely why I have chosen to be practically oriented in this academic venture that addresses the basic need of man. Just as Keating, referring to suffering once more, observed:

> *Suffering is never an end in itself, but a stepping-stone to transformation. In this view it may be a necessary step to focus on us, to let go of what we overly depend on for the fulfillment of our idea of happiness (Keating, Thomas. 2000:24).*

As we already noted in the course of this writing, the importance of psychology in everyday life, even in our suffering moments, is part and parcel of anthropological advancements. Based on the various materials and books we reviewed above in chapter two of this book, the management strategies and skills necessary for this work of counseling are evident. The application of such skills demands a professional approach cum my experiences as a Certified Nurse. At this juncture, my encounter with this particular patient who reminded me of the painful experiences of my few friends in Nigeria, as noted already, stampeded me into the PhD Program within this area of study. As it were, the methodology adopted and employed for this scientific investigation will be entirely descriptive, narrative, and practically evidenced as presented in this book.

Eventually, after I visited a pregnant woman, whose only male child was lying critically at a quack clinic because there were no resources to take him to a good hospital, I felt wounded myself. On entering the room, while she was not looking at the baby, her other elderly child was leaning on the so-called hospital bed as if she was so tired to stand. The situation looked sad. Thus, in this contextual analysis, the picture of the said woman was not physically cited here, but the memory of what I observed was the spring board on which the research methodology was built and circled. Imagine the picture or photo of a pregnant woman with another baby lying critically on the bed. Is that not enough to elicit a research of this magnitude? Metaphorically, a closer examination of the woman is a big picture of what so many others are going through in their lives on daily basis. In fact, this was basically the last struck that broke the camel's back and led me to this inquiry in order to acquire more basic tools and skills I need to address their needs. The issue is not a laughing one.

The Research Design and Outline:

Number of Visits	2
Patient's name	Mary AB (Not the real name at all)
Age	44
Sex	Female
Race	White
Admission	N/A
Diagnosis	Spinal dislocation
Religion	Catholic
Marriage Status	Married
Occupation	Registered Nurse
Location	Unit - N/A
Date of visits	7/29/10 & 7/30/10
Length of time	1hr. 10 min

Reasons for choosing the present case

In the Bible, Jesus said, "I have told you this so that you might have peace in me. In the world you will have trouble, but take courage, I have conquered the world" (John 16:33). The question that arose in my mind was, "Did Jesus' victory include everybody, or were some exempted?" It is consoling that Jesus explained that a person's suffering or problem is not necessarily caused by his or her sins, or even that of his or her immediate parents, but that God will nonetheless make use of suffering as long as it exists to achieve his purpose with humankind (John 9: 1-3). I strongly buy the view that, although there are different degrees of suffering and also some positive aspects or experiences in life that we perceive as the opposite of suffering, such as ease, comfort and happiness, life in its totality is imperfect and incomplete. The case at hand is pitiable.

All the same, my denominational aim for choosing this course of study was parallel or similar to the case a fellow nurse had. This nurse lost her job due to incapacitation resulting from spinal injuries she sustained sometime in her place of work and the impact the loss had on her family as a whole. Such horrible encounter still compels me to deepen my passion and concern for those who have similar cases. It is my uttermost intention to explore the rich value of psychology in dealing with such human problems and suffering. As a nurse and Counselor, as indicated in my ministry statement, I am challenged to examine most of the emotional problems that create stress, frustration, grief, suicide, and untimely death for people in society today.

Again, this woman under review was friendly to my close friend at the time of this visit or encounter in my hospital. Therefore, the encounter presented here was dimensional which I made myself. The impact such similar encounters had made in my life were tremendously instrumental to my choice of Program and Profession.

It is my aspiration and passion to professionally learn the best ways I can be helpful to other people in various emotional crises.

Patient's Background

Patient was a white young lady of 44 years old. She was married and her husband of 56 years was sick at home and patient alone took care of herself. Her initial concern when I approached her was the situation of her husband and children. They have two kids, a son and a daughter of 19 and 16 respectively, who are living outside the States. This very patient happened to be an X-Nun before she got married. She was anxious to go home and be there for her sick husband but her spinal cord injury made it impossible. The patient was also a registered nurse.

Preparation and Contemplation for visiting the patient

One of our social workers informed me of this particular case and how loving the patient was. Actually, the social worker is a friend of mine with whom I had shared faith stories and pleasantries. But on this fateful day when she told me of the situation of Mary AB, she wanted me to keep her in my prayers. Some of the nurses call me "Mary's daughter" because they often see me praying the Rosary. However, as a nurse, I have patients specifically assigned to me. Unless there are emergencies that can compel me to render a helping hand to patients other than mine, my attention is always focused on the ones assigned to me. On my first visit to this patient, I simply went there to greet her because of the good things the social worker had told me about her. I knew she was Catholic but she did not know that I specifically came into that room to greet her. But after I introduced myself as a Catholic nurse in the hospital, she asked me if I could send for a Catholic chaplain to bring her the Holy Communion or Eucharist.

Having being a Eucharistic Minister in my former Parish or Church, I promised to bring her the Holy Communion. She was so excited to hear that I was a Eucharistic minister and would bring her the Eucharist myself. However, I did not stay long with her because I was getting ready to go for the day and the hospital Bus driver was already waiting to give us a ride. It was on the second day of my visit when I came to give her the Holy Communion that this patient opened up to me and narrated her story or ordeal to me. It was an apogee of psychological encounter. I had wanted to see the patient first thing in the morning before I started my shifts. I had not even dressed up for work. I had my jacket on, my bag and just wanted to give her the Holy Communion and get to the day's work.

When I knocked on her door and showed my face in greetings, her therapist was with her. They were 2 patients in that room and her bed was by the window. Then I excused myself and promised to come back shortly to give her the Holy Communion. She had wanted to interrupt and stop the therapist immediately she saw me and receive the Holy Communion if I had not begged and promised to come back. Within few hours I had reported to work, I horridly went back to the same patient and this time, a doctor was with her. I did not want to keep the Eucharist in my bag for so long because of its sacredness. Unfortunately, it turned out that I kept the Eucharist in my bag all day. I felt nervous, guilty and did not know how I was going to explain or confess to our pastor for keeping the Eucharist in my bag at work place. However, I did not let anyone know of it or touch my bag.

Luckily, I waited patiently till my break time. Few minutes to my break time, I made for her room, ready to give her the Eucharist and go for me break. But it did not work out that way. On the contrary, it turned out that I spent my entire break hour with her. When I came in with the Eucharist, not only did she see the pix or container of the Eucharist, but she also knew I was about to start praying in preparation for the reception of the Eucharist. But she did not show any sign of receiving the Eucharist at that moment and started to express and share her concerns and feelings with me. As a professional, it is always more therapeutic to follow the patients from where they are or their lead than forcing your ministry on them. Administration of medication is a bit different. Yet, every patient has the freedom and right to accept treatment or refuse. At a point I felt like interrupting her in order to accomplish few engagements during my break. As I said earlier, this time again, it did not turn out that way. I was initially shocked that this patient who requested for the Holy Communion did not mention it throughout my stay with her.

My Encounter and Observation with her at that moment

There were two patients in the room and they were all white ladies of about the same age. A large curtain demarcated the two beds. Mary AB was lying on her back and her face was beaming with smile, which continued throughout the time of my visit. Her physical appearance did not show she was suffering any spinal cord injury or in great pain. Her corner was so neat and she looked so bright in appearance. But as a nurse, I could observe she was really in pain. Nothing proved to me that many family members or friends have been visiting her because there were no gift cards, flowers, and baskets of fruits. As soon as I came in, she managed to shift position, trying to raise the upper part of her bed up to interact with me. I knew she was so happy to see me come back the second day and the third time, that day. She was able to communicate verbally. We had the following conversation:

Conversation

M = Patient (Mary AB), **N** = Nurse (Myself):

N1 Hello M, I hope you are doing okay

M1 So-so my friend, I can't complain

N2 I am Christy, one of the nurses in this hospital, you have seen me before

M2 Yes Christy, you were here yesterday, am I right, thanks so much for coming to visit me (*smiling*). My husband is sick at home and my two kids don't live around us. I am alone here, as it were.

N3 That sounds so frustrating that you are here alone.

M3 It is. You can't believe the nature of pains I experience on my back because of my spinal cord dislocation. If you watch me, I cannot sit properly but simply lie on my back. I strongly believe that the omnipotent God will see me through.

N4 I pray God grants your request. Mrs. M, why can't your children come here to visit you since they are grown-ups. Though, you don't look sick except that you are here in the hospital.

M 4 Christy, my appearance is deceptive; I have been in a great pain for quite a long period of time now. I have had this awful back pain for some years and I have gone through one surgery to another surgery. I have had seven surgeries in four years and my situation is not getting any better. Christy, I am tired of staying in the hospital. I want to get out of here. I have been here for almost eight months, in and out of the hospital. I want to go home and take care of my husband who has been very sick for many years now. I miss him; he cannot come here and there is no way anybody could bring him down to see me. I was a registered nurse and used to take care of him. Sickness has forced me to retire, and now, I can't do much for myself, let alone for him. I really want to go home. My beautiful children have visited once and they call me on the phone most often. You know how our system works here. They are all working. I miss them too *(at this time, patient who has maintained a smiling face as she narrated her stories, began frowning).*

N5 You are really going through a lot. Sorry to hear all that. I know you love your family, should you go home under pain?

M5 I have missed my family so much. Imagine I have been in this hospital almost one year now. Eight months are not eight days. I hear there are chaplains in this hospital; I have only seen one on two different occasions. The doctors, nurses and my physical therapists are always here. I don't like complaining. I am tired of staying here. I watch the Mass at the TV *(pointing to the hanging Television in her room)*. Do you still want to hear more *(laughing aloud)*?

N6 Sure! That will be nice if you have the time. I am happy to be here.

M6 I left my religious profession after 10 years and married for 25 years *(she laughs)*, my husband is 56 and this is why I don't want to leave him alone. He married me when I was 27 years. I entered the religious life at 17 and since then I have remained a religious at heart in whatever I do.

N7 You have nice memory. What does being religious at heart mean for you?

M7 I was a Nun for 10 years. I loved the religious life until the time Nuns started to put off their habits and lived outside the convent on their own. I hated the changes in the religious houses and so I decided to quit. I got married and our marriage was blessed with a son and a daughter. But despite my marriage, I have always devoted myself to the Eucharist, praying my Rosary as we used to do in the convent and I try to be nice to people. Every member of my family prays the Rosary every day and loves our Lady, the Blessed Virgin Mary. I still remember the love we shared together in the convent. Religious lives are more secluded and cloistered than the family ones. There is discipline in both marriage and religious life, depending on what one wants. I am not making a comparison. I love my marriage.

N8 Wow! What a blessing then!

M8 Our children are away from us and we have been living alone for many years, though, they visit from time to time. How I wished the doctor would discharge me soon because I feel better now. This has been the longest period we have been without each other since our marriage. I am so sorry I have taken much of your time today. Will you come again Christy? Please, before you leave, can we say some prayers?

N9 Obviously, it is my pleasure to be here and share your stories. I thank you very much and I will come to visit you again. Let us begin our prayer "In the name of the Father, and of the Son, and of the Holy Spirit. Amen!" Lord, I pray that you discharge my friend, Mary AB soon as she had wished and I will continue to pray for her family, husband and children, through Christ our Lord. Amen!" Thank you Mary AB and peace be with you. (As *I try to leave, she smiles and adds):*

M 9 and also with you Christy

CHAPTER FOUR

 ～√～

ANALYSIS, EVALUATION AND INTERPRETATION OF FIRST VALUE ENGAGEMENT WITH PATIENT – THE PREGNANT WOMAN, FAMILY AND MARY AB

A. Analysis of the picture of the family I visited:

According to Morgan:

Attentiveness to guiding process of inquiry guides one to seek progressively understand, value, act and love. Ultimately, each person is capable of this movement toward self-transcendence because he or she is by nature a questioner: "transcendence is the elementary matter of raising further questions (Morgan, H. John. 2009:99).

Unlike what Morgan has noted above, when the guiding process of an inquiry is clouded with indescribable events or situations, the capability for this movement towards self-transcendence makes the questioner speechless. Yet within the transcendent experience, one may raise more questions as necessary. As it were, the above picture presents a great challenge and deep concern for the questioning and inquiring counselors. Perceptions deceive at times. In the imaginary but real photograph to me, a lot of interpretations could be given. It is possible that the woman has her sick baby boy, but that may not be the whole story. The issue at hand is not as limited to what is observed here than the reality we must admit.

This is a woman whose tranquility of life appears distracted and disturbed by events beyond her control. In the first place, the fact that she was not looking at her sick baby indicates a situation of hopelessness, desperation and melancholy. She does not even seem to be communicating with any person in that picture. Despite the fact that there was a young girl there who, we supposedly guessed to be her older child, suggested an unimaginable worst state of life. Further analysis of her present environment, call it, a health facility did not give joy either. The hospital or clinical environment, so to say, did not look professional. Her baby was just lying on a piece of cloth, which indicated that the bed had no proper bedding or materials to make a sick person comfortable. That cloth appeared to belong to her. What do I say of the blood transfusion bag I saw there? It was just hanging on the window without any stand of its own? Assuming that we draw our conclusion based on the facts presented to our analysis, only God knows the level of care and healing that could occur in such a facility. Within the few hours I spent with this woman, no Dr. or nurse came in to check on her sick baby. Even the posture of her older child called for immediate attention, because the child herself appeared troubled and dehydrated not only by her sibling's situation, but also by her personal matters.

At a first value evaluation, we might conclude that those in the picture are there for the sickness of the child that is lying on the bed. But, when we go a little bit further, there is every indication that the family involved here is sick too. I know that sickness takes people to different countries while the people involved remain physically on site. Actually, there is no gainsaying that the woman and her children are so devastated that coming to the hospital provides them some sort of support. Only God knows how they will feel when they are asked to go home or discharged from that hospital. The pregnant woman herself seems to have need for medical attention too. However, it is impossible to conclude whether the family in this picture has a home or not, judging from what is presented before us. In any case, what is important is that there are so many people worse than what we may imagine in the present case. For instance, the pregnant woman needs to be approached by a professional to find out how she feels besides being around her sick child. Sickness speaks more languages than can be understood ordinarily. I need to become a counselor in order to find the best ways I can be of great assistance to people like the ones in the above picture.

B. The Second Analysis with Mary AB:

My visit with the patient in the above conversation revealed another form of desperation people go through in their lives. It is not enough to conclude that Mary AB is in the hospital with spinal dislocations and stop at that when the psychological issues around her are enormous and need some professional attention. That is why my encounter with the patient is dimensional and educating. I really established a pastoral relationship with patient. I felt I had made the best use of my break hour by this unique visit. My client, as it were, was happy too. The visit revealed as noted above that a patient in the hospital could be sick of other issues other than the ones known, diagnosed and treated by doctors, hence, the need for our enquiry in this book, "Beyond the iceberg".

Actually this patient had back pain due to her spinal dislocation but she was so worried about her husband's sickness. The issue of her husband's sickness and her missing him dominated greater part of our conversation, which meant she was suffering from other pains other than the ones she was being treated for, in the hospital. The fact that patient and husband lived alone without their kids because they lived outside the State. far away from them was a form of sickness also. Most often, doctors and medical personnel may not know what a patient is going through while in the hospital and most of them have no time to find out. Diagnosis in similar situations will always defile all administrations of medication.

Eventually, the case takes me home concerning the issue that arose when my best friend left the Catholic Church and joined the Pentecostals. Because we were so close to each other, some people thought I was going to quit the Church too. Her leaving the Catholic faith did not prevent us being friends, though with some issues to discuss about. The events of the time came back to my memory. Mary AB, the patient of my discussion has much strength from the Sacraments, in her faith community. She spoke of the chaplains not coming to visit her regularly. She expressed her devotion to the Eucharist and Sacraments generally, but did not ask or remind me to give her the Holy Communion she had ab initio sent for. It is really revealing that companionship or supportive presence could mean much to the sick people generally than anything else on the planet.

Evaluation of Psychological and Pastoral Skills:

1.   Listening skills:

From that visit, I felt I had listened more than I talked. Attentive listening skills are so important in every human interaction and counseling. To listen to people is to value and respect them. However one thinks or feels affects how one lives and acts (Capuzzi & Gross, 2003:219). Thus, when someone or a sick person knows you are ready to listen to him, then he brightens up for your company. On the other hand, unwillingness to listen is an indication of apathy. Hardly does healing occur from medical professionals who do not listen to the sick or family member.

2. Availability skills:

It was good I did not postpone visiting Mary AB till the next day. The need for follow up visits and interaction on appointments with a patient who has emotional problems is necessary. In this particular case study, Mary AB seemed to complain about the chaplains who were not visiting her because she needed a group of people to hear her pains. It was on account of that too that she expressed her worry about the absence of her family members while she was there.

3. Assessment skills:

My empathetic responses assisted the patient to open up to me. I allowed her to play a leading role in that visit. Most often, when we, the nurses and doctors visit patients or sick people, we assume to be in control, their masters, and dish out what we think is good for them without caring more on how they feel about us. In this particular case, I visited Mary as a friend, bringing Jesus to her without any reference to my expertise or profession as a nurse.

4. Non-judgmental skills:

I knew the patient had asked me to bring her the Eucharist. I had expected her to ask for it, but I allowed her to make her choice without claiming to know what she needed or her feelings were. There is a big difference between imagining how people feel and claiming to know what or how they feel. Only the individual person knows how he or she feels. To engage in any conversation with a person who has an issue, like being sick, there is need to allow the person express his feelings and not imagining or forcing him to adopt your own position. For instance, that Mary AB's situation reminded me of a similar case with another person I knew was quite a different case or story. Mary's case is unique and must be treated that way.

5. Non-argumentative skills:

Mary was in control of that conversation. I allowed her to freely express herself and her values without asserting my own values or myself. My passion for the sick and willingness to assist them compel me to place their conveniences and well-being first before my own without compromising my professional ethics – administering medication when appropriate and due, at times, whether the patient might want it or not. Yet, the manner a doctor or nurse approaches a patient makes a difference. As professional, we must avoid forcing medication to patients or ignoring their complaints even if we must administer medication to them. That is why, the need for "TAMAP" (Trained and Approved Medication Administration Personnel) is essential in clinical settings. The tone of voices should be considered too in administering medication to sick people. Once a patient realizes that the doctor or nurse is there for his welfare and recovery, he calms down whenever he sees him or her, the nature of pain notwithstanding.

6. Self-awareness skills:

I did not plan staying long with Mary. But as a professional I am, I listened to her patiently without creating the impression that it was my break time or that I wanted to accomplish other tasks that day. This is wisdom, God-given gift to know what is right and doing it. Hence, the book of wisdom says, "Watch for her early and you will have no trouble; you will find her sitting at your gates" (Wisdom

6:14-15). I applied this emotional intelligence or intellectual virtue on that my visit and left the patient rejuvenated and energized.

7.   Priority goal-setting skills:

Actually, I came to bring the Eucharist to Mary. But realizing her interest in my visit, I felt the need to give her the supportive presence she needed without imposition of any sort. My visit that day was so therapeutic that I knew in my heart, that some healings have been accomplished in the patient, which is the goal of psychology and practice.

8.   Association skills:

I did not need to be told that my encounter with Mary was fundamental and educational in the process of psychotherapy and clients. In other words, my personal evaluation and experiences with this particular case or patient can always form the basis for attending to other similar cases.

9.   Client-oriented skills:

Juxtaposing my assessment of Mary AB's expressions, my visit that day and my practice as a registered nurse, one basic factor is evident. That is, I have come to the conclusion that much emphasis should be placed on the welfare of clients or patients first, before the convenience of the medical practitioners. The implication is, doctors and nurses should keep their personal emotions aside and approach sick people with care, dedication, and love and avoid placing emphasis on their paychecks. If, for no other reason, a person who claims to be sick has admitted his helplessness and the need to be taken care of.

10. Functional and momentary skills:

Every medical professional should always try and find out what patients, clients and their families need at the moment. It is true that one comes to hospital to be cured. All sicknesses are not subject to diagnosis. There are so many issues, as noted already; which sick people go through at their beds in the hospital that are beyond medical science. There are unresolved issues, crisis, losses and disappointments many people carry with them to the hospital walls. No wonder Nwachukwu remarks that "Unresolved issues color personal feelings" (Nwachukwu, 2011:5).

Therefore, doctors and nurses should be careful in dealing with sick people who come to them for help. Any effort made to find out what bothers a patient or sick person at initial visit is important for the healing process. The simple implication is that doctors and nurses should not mind or take to heart when sick people yell at them in the hospital, while or when they are trying to treat them.

The patient had confidence in and trusted me with her stories. Many Ex- Nuns I know try to hide their identity and would not allow people know that they left the religious life. Some do not even like to be associated with the Church any more due to their unresolved personal issues. But Mary AB opened up and told me everything about her past life, her relationship with other Nuns in the convent, her husband and their children. I did not doubt that she left the religious life in good fate or loved her husband and was happy with her marriage. As noted, both of us seemed to have forgotten her sickness or spinal dislocation in the moment and shared values that energized progress and health. At various moments in our discussion, we felt we just met as friends and not like on professional level, nurse-client relationship. Healing took place on both sides in that visit because while patient felt relieved by my visit, I was, on the other hand, encouraged and edified by her fortitude and perseverance.

The Interpretation of Findings:

i. Pastoral

Mary AB's first response "so-so my friend, I can't complain" to my greetings when I was trying to find out how she was doing, had a lot to say about what she was going through in her life. The response indicated she needed some assistance because she was feeling upset. The "so-so" was in line with the primary concern she expressed and her second utterance "my husband is sick at home and my two kids don't live around us. I am alone here". Those were the catching emotional words that, not only energized my being there to offer continued supportive presence, but also that touched my heart to give her undivided attention that day. At the end of that visit, I promised to visit her again the next day. Again, my prayer-points and promise to continue praying for her and her loving family [husband and children] pointed to my pastoral plan.

ii. Religious/Theological

Mrs. Mary AB had great faith in God and strongly believed in prayers, the Eucharist and ministers of the sacraments, the chaplains. She knew I was a laywoman, yet she went ahead and requested for Holy Communion from me. The depth or magnitude of her faith was expressed in M3, when she alluded to God's omnipotence over the excruciating pains she sustained from her back due to the spinal dislocation. She had great love for God too. Nothing can be more theological than living out one's love of God among other people, even in pains. Generally, my visit and encounter with Mary AB spoke clearly about the true love of husband and wife. It is like the love Christ has for His body, the Church. The theological implication of my visit is likened to the Love of Christ and his Church or simply put, 'love of neighbor'.

When Christ faced his death on the cross, amidst mockery and laughter, he forgave his executioners. Here, Mary AB was not so much worried about her spinal dislocation but the situation of her sick husband and absence of her children. Love is solidified more at sickness when there are uncertainties of what could happen to a family member that is sick. This is agape in the true sense of it. God so loved the world that he gave his begotten son to die" (John 3:16) for those he loved. There at her sick bed, Mary AB was equally in pain for her love for her family. The theology of hope is made explicit here too. Mary AB has great anticipation in the unfailing love of God, come rain and come sun, God would not abandon her and her family.

iii. Social-Economic

It was easy for me to know exactly the social status of the patient. Her level of relationship and interaction with me was clear. She brought in family issues, her life at home as an X-Nun, a caring mother and good wife. She felt comfortable with her marriage and never complained of money or such related matters throughout our discussion. Mary AB was human and simple, despite her sickness, always appreciating my visit. Her openness to my visit gave me a lot of motivation to listen to her and I felt I had more time to spend with her.

iv. Psychological/Emotional

I have already noted the therapeutic effects of my visit. The patient felt she was cured of her sickness. Imagine a discussion of one hour and few minutes, both of us felt comfortable with each other in a hospital. The fact that she forgot to ask of the Eucharist that meant much to her because of my presence alone was the height of it all. We were emotionally connected to a point that she wanted me come again and I promised to visit the next day. There are so many other things we could deduce from my visit and interaction with Mary AB. Besides the very sickness that brought someone to hospital, the sick person may have other burning issues that cannot be handled by doctors and nurses but religiously or spiritually. Here lies the need for psychological practice in our society today.

CHAPTER FIVE

~~∿~~

SUMMARY OF WORK

We started this work by stating the importance and value of psychology and psychological practice in the life of individuals and society. By psychological practice we mean the application of specific branches of psychology to real life situation. It took into account how my profession as a nurse could affect and influence the healing process of the sick and the healthy. This research centered on the incorporation of psychology and practice into solving people's problems, especially within the area of counseling psychology. The question bothered on what I intended to achieve as a counselor or pastoral counselor or psychologist.

That was why in chapter one of this book, we examined the statement of problems, outlining the 4 parameters involved. In a sense, these parameters assisted us to shape the nature of the work at hand – the background of study, purpose, and scope and significance of study. In the background, we discovered that society had suffered a lot of frustrations, traumas, and unforeseen setbacks because of lack of proper directions. The manner in which people behave affects them in various aspects of their lives, psychological, emotional and even religiously. There is need to assist people focus on important priorities in life. That was actually what led us to the purpose of the work. People need to be directed on issues that surround them. For instance, a person who does not know at what point the rain started beating him may not know at what point it stopped. There are so many unresolved issues people go through in their lives.

Therefore, any efforts made to assist them resolve these issues, consciously or unconsciously is of paramount importance. Our scope was defined as much emphasis was placed on the Nigerian people, particularly Umuokirika Ekwereazu, Imo State of Nigeria, due to the stressful situations they go through because of poor government. Only God knows the extent these people have suffered today because of hardship resulting from lack of the basic amenities of life and infrastructures.

There is no employment of the youths after schooling. Some have joined or turned into armed robbery and kidnapping. The stress has become so evident that someone could be walking along the road aimlessly without taking notice of passing cars. Some have died in the process. Hence, our emphasis was centered on that part of the globe. The significance of this book lies on the good news it is going to bring to the people. At least, for no other reasons, this book will challenge the government and give some hopes to the people. That is to say, once this problem-solving material is made available to the people and it helps them cope with their situations, then, it has become significant and relevant to the situation at hand.

The chapter two of this work was a bit voluminous. In this chapter, we consulted and examined the works of few great psychologists, psychotherapists, and psychiatrists and some topical materials in the area of psychological practice. Along this line of argument, we treated and featured 4 specific professionals whose materials we extensively employed in the development of this book.

First and foremost, we studied the "Therapeutic dynamics of psychology in theory and practice". Without over flogging the issue as already discussed in this book, there is need for psychology in everyday life. As a human science, psychology takes care of human behaviors and actions and the evaluations of such mannerisms. Theoretically, there can be basic psychology that studies different aspects of life that lacks application to real human problems. Psychology becomes applicable when it aims at solving practical and particular human needs and problems here and now. Mentalist-based knowledge of psychology is not always the best of it. Psychology should be practical by assisting people in their plights. For instance, a sick person needs care and cure at the same time. When care does not precede cure, there is a problem. In caring for people, most often, they get cured from their ailments, hence the need for psychological practice in our time today.

Counseling psychology is skillfully related to pastoral counseling for ministry professionals. Our emphasis is on the Ekwereazu Umuokirika, Imo State of Nigeria. As noted at the scope of this work, our investigation here is of universal significance. Time has come when those who claim to offer one form of ministry or the other have to employ the best skills for effective results. Ministers have to lead by examples of their professionalism. By ministers here, we include all those who bring one form of compassion and healing to the needy, physical and emotional, handicapped, dejected of society or sick in the hospital, including counseling psychologists. There are so many problems besieging society that cannot be treated in the hospital. Therefore, ministry should not be limited to the Church, the clergy, pastors and the religious or ministers of different religions. There are other ministry professionals other than those associated with traditional ministry of the Church. For instance, a medical doctor or surgeon or nurse in the hospital can be a better minister to a sick person than a minister of the Church or religion. What is important is the manner of approach of the minister to the needy. As a Eucharistic minister and nurse, my visit to Mary AB as noted above meant more than the Eucharist I brought to her. That is why my choice of career is different from being a dedicated ministry professional and counseling psychologist or simply put, a Counselor. Pastoral counseling is determined by the manner of each ministry professional and not by the hood or wears of a pastor, as studies and experiences have shown.

We equally studied the thoughts and works of Carl Ransom Rogers and his person-centered psychotherapy. When we speak of the need for psychological practice in society, we are inevitably compelled to examine the works of Carl Rogers. This man has been noted as the grandfather of modern pastoral psychologist and the father of person-centered psychotherapy. He made the individual person at the moment the center of his academic investigation. For him, respect for the individual person is not only unique, but also the center of all anthropological studies.

People tend to behave true to type. Having come from a disciplined family background, I saw Christianity as a unique force in human nature and believe that hard work is more important than ritualistic and legalistic endeavors. Carl Rogers believes that no human person is useless. Rather; each person has the inclination to become the best he is naturally meant to be. There is need to give everybody a second chance. Person-centered psychotherapy is primarily concerned with the best of the individual person. A doctor, nurse, or psychologist needs not to lord it over his client because the sick or client is the center of all medical attention, comfort, care and not the other way round. Finally, Rogers encourages the individual to build self-confidence in him or herself and work hard to achieve the best and success life provides.

Another psychologist or thought we studied here was Harry Stack Sullivan and his interpersonal psychoanalysis. This is another psychologist who has shown the need for psychological practice – application of psychology to the various areas of need. He is well known as the father of modern psychiatry. For him, nobody is an island. We need one another to be and live. We need interpersonal relations. He suffered the loneliness of his time, especially from his family background, and now advocates for interpersonal relationships. He was not so much a Churchgoer or fanatical about faith but he willed to be buried as Catholic. In other words, it does not matter much what Church one goes to, or the religion one believes in, the most important thing is that, one has a place to go after here. This fact compels us to lead good lives.

He shared the same view with Carl Rogers that no human life is useless. Give people the chance to show their worth. For him, education and success depend on hard work and not on family background alone. He did not rule out the part family could play in the education of her children. Relationship, which is therapeutic, should not always be based on professional levels but by being human. Each person needs to be studied, approached as a whole and not in parts. Psychiatry should not be limited to administration of medication but based on the manner in which the professional approaches his clients.

We also studied the life and works of Erik Erikson. In his highly acclaimed, *Childhood and Society*, according to Morgan, "Erikson identified and extensively elaborated upon a sequence of eighth separate stages of psychosocial ego development, what was usually in shorthand fashion referred to as the 'eight stages of man'" (Morgan, 2010:144). The effect society and parents have on the development of each child is clearly treated by Erikson as we studied previously. In a very dramatic way, Morgan states that, "For Erikson, the psychosocial stages of ego development were chronologically sequenced and each was accompanied with a "crisis" component which could work either positively or negatively" (Ibid). These eight stages of man in his personality developments are the high water marks of his study and contribution to society.

Again, Alfred Adler was another important psychologist studied in this work, especially his individual, child psychology. According to Morgan, "Adler never stopped emphasizing the need to stimulate into the child a sense of confidence, to evoke his cooperative dispositions, to socialize and humanize his ego, especially to teachers and parents" (Morgan, 2010:59). That is why the positive life style of partners, guardians, and parents is as important as life itself. Children build self-confidence from the positive life patterns of those around them.

The chapter three of this work was a personal dimensional case study and experiences and my impression of the photo under analysis, especially of the professional visit I made to a patient, Mary AB, who sent for the Eucharist. It was initially unplanned. I was a Eucharistic minister but never had I done so in my hospital. A friend of mine, a social worker had told me of the loving woman in question and how nice she was to all who came across her and I promised to visit her. That was the starting point of the development of this book coupled with my earlier experiences in my village regarding a very close friend of mine who suffered back injuries and lost her job as a result. That was precisely my main reason for choosing this case study.

The background of the 44-year-old white lady who had 2 children and sick husband was noted. As earlier observed, my preparation and contemplation for the visit came about through a friend, social worker who told me to go and pray for the nice lady in question. I feel blessed to be associated with prayer and as being very close to God in whatever I do. I am popularly known in my hospital as "Mary's daughter" because I often hold and pray my Rosary during my free times. Actually, my friend had asked me to send for a Catholic chaplain for the said patient for the Holy Communion. Being a Eucharistic minister myself, once in my Church, I opted to go and visit the patient and bring her the Holy Communion. My encounter and observation of the patient were enriching enough. A visit I thought would last for less than 5 minutes turned into an hour and ten minutes altogether.

It was amazing. I had a wonderful conversation with her and from the fruits of that conversation; I was able to underline a lot of materials that assisted me in this research or book. Besides, my analysis of the pregnant African woman and her sick baby was an eye opener. That picture alone stimulated my passion to investigate more on the possible professional manners I could come to the aid of people of such situations. The situation at hand reminded me of the famous Ancient Roman Poet Virgil who was said, "Sunt lacrimae in rerum", which means, "There are tears in the things of life". It was an elucidation of what Pope John Paul 11 once stated in the following words:

> Suffering is something which is still wider than sickness, more complex and at the same time still more deeply rooted in humanity itself. A certain idea of this problem comes to us from the distinction between physical suffering and moral suffering (Pope Paul 11, Salvifici Doloris, On the Christian meaning of Human suffering, 1984, no. 5).

I do not doubt that suffering is deep rooted in humanity as Pope John Paul 11 expressed it. On a very different note, the analysis, evaluation, interpretation and pastoral engagement of my visit in chapter four of this work were interesting. The manner in which the unplanned conversation took place assisted me in assessing my own skills in dealing with people of this nature. According to Morgan's views, "One has at least an opportunity to shape one's own identity to create oneself" (Morgan, 1987:38), but not in the sense of humanistic philosophies. For Sartre maintained that, "Man is nothing else but what he makes of himself". I strongly believe that man can go ahead to develop himself in the ways he desires to live his life or make it more meaningful, provided that his desires do not infringe upon the grand plan God has for him.

Eventually, it was based on the above position that Morgan, responding to Carl Barth's views in his 'The Humanity of God' said, "Mankind cannot come to know of the humanity of God's deity except in Jesus Christ. With Jesus Christ, we are confronted with God incarnate in human flesh....But in Jesus Christ, God is not apart from man, nor man apart from God" (Morgan, 1987:77). Morgan commenting on the position of Barth's 'The Humanity of God,' made it clear that the relationship that exists between God and man is abundantly interwoven. As it were, Morgan further summarized the work of Barth in a more concrete terms, in these words, "For in Jesus Christ, it is established once and for all eternity that God does not exist without man" (Morgan 1987:78-79), to honor and glorify him.

The patient I encountered seemed to be in charge of that conversation. In my evaluation of my psychological and pastoral skills, I felt that day that I developed more listening skills, availability skills, non-judgmental, argumentative, client-centered orientation, and needed to be with others in the moment skills etc. Within the area of interpretation, the pastoral implication was that the patient needed my presence more than the Sacrament. On the religious level, any religion that is excluded from interpersonal relationship is baseless. Most often, we find God in our neighbors. The social-economic aspect of the visit was manifested in the sense that the patient loved her family so much and saw me as one of them since the scenario did not show she had visitors or family members visit her in the hospital. On the psychological and emotional level, I saw that the patient was a human being, who interacted with me as such. Counseling session works and succeeds fast with an open-minded client. As the case at hand, the patient looked beyond her pains and sickness and shared pertinent stories and life values with me. And that made her feel stronger and healthier at that moment of my visit.

Chapter six of my enquiry was also a form of evaluation in which I analyzed the outcomes of my visit. This is where the researcher could not have claimed to exhaust the whole issues related with the need for psychology in our times and lives. There are yet other areas or works to be accomplished within this topic. It will be left to other prospective researchers to carry out or investigate into them. As it were, the limitation of this book was outlined along with its educational implications.

The chapter seven of this book was precisely the acknowledgment of our resources or bibliography. There is always the need to honestly indicate the sources, names of authors and experts whose works were cited or used in developing a book or research work. That was what we did in this chapter. The final chapter as such was the appendices and glossary of terms where foreign or unfamiliar words were explained.

CHAPTER SIX

✑

WORK YET TO BE DONE

In a research work or book such as this, it is very hard for a candidate to claim to have done all the works that needed to be carried out in the same related area. For instance, other students are to investigate on other aspects of the area of our study, "Applying the value of psychology in other areas of life, including various organizations, companies, in schools, government quarters, and cases for pastoral, socio-religious reasons et cetera". There are horizons for research in these related areas of the need for psychology, such as that of industries, market, trading, sports, agriculture and what have you. When they do so, they are going to view it differently by subtracting and adding flesh to the ones we have done here. Therefore, in this chapter, we are compelled to state our limitations and the educational implications of what we have done already and recommendations for further studies. We are briefly going to summarize this section in this order:

A. Limitation of study

The need for psychology in human life is such that humanity cannot exist without it. It is of classic importance and global in content. But the book seemed to have limited it to the Nigerian situation, with particular emphasis on her tribe, the Igbo of Nigeria, Umuokirika in

Ekwerazu, Imo State. Most of the examples drawn here were from the same remote area that is somehow oblivious of other countries that have recourse to the need for psychology. For instance, if "psychological practice" concerns the application of the various aspects of human person, his thoughts, aspirations, decisions, choices and actions, to everyday life, then this topic should have involved a global discussion. Besides, a topic like this should discuss the use of politics, religion, culture, economy, and education in the development of the human person. Except that some experts we consulted mentioned all these in passing, attention should have been given to them in no less measure. Delving into the hidden life of others is an uphill task. We cannot guarantee 100% success in our findings and conclusions.

Today, lots of messes are being made on the drug industry due to materialistic tendencies. This work should have highlighted some ways of curbing them. What of on the religious circles, most ministers of God's Word use the media to make astronomical gains for themselves and their families and not for leading people to God. The area of psychological practice, its value, whether it is from pastoral perspective or not, is such a wide one that should incorporate and unite the Church, government and society. Until this unity is achieved, there is still a loophole on the part of this book. In many quarters of society, there are chaos, stress, ill feelings, squabbles, sufferings, craziness for worldly ambitions, lack of trust in marriage circles, broken friendships and homes, indiscipline among teenage boys and girls and what have you. The point is that a topic such as this should have harnessed the various capabilities and potentials of the individual person and channeled them to the right values for authentic actions and behaviors. But from the evidence and happenings in society, there are so many troubles besieging humanity, which this book could have addressed. The fact that it did not do so, points to its limitations as well.

However, the book seemed to have advanced more on the area of counseling needs of an individual traumatized with emotional problems instead of its social, religious, economic and political aspects. Even from the case study, it is easy to understand the line of thought and argument of this book. Addressing and studying the individuals with emotional needs, the sick, the needy of society have not said it all because at times, a person who claims to be in need may only be deceiving the general public. At times, the statement, "I am sick or I have a need" may be relative defiling all quantifications and qualifications. In Umuokirika Ekwerazu, for example, a person who claims to be sick may prefer to be given physical cash to consulting a medical doctor or going to the hospital. Consequently, here lies the need for other researchers to dig deep into this topic and address those areas the book did not handle. At this point, there is need to outline the educational implication of this book.

B. Educational implication of work

The extensive works done on the area of psychological practice and value of psychology as a case for counseling in this book have so many implications for society to self-supervise itself. Besides the fact that almost the experts on psychology we consulted here have their personal messages for educational growth, we shall enumerate the educational implications of this book and outline them in this order:

i. The therapeutic nature of psychology is adequate to guide the human person. "Man know thyself" is a popular aphorism that needs to be understood by everybody. Looking into one's inner life is the beginning of personal healing, the power manifestation of each person;

ii. The issue of ministry should be extended to include social workers, doctors, nurses, and various caregivers, counselors who sincerely approach the human person, sick or healthy with respect, love and compassion;

iii. Days are gone when only the ministers, pastors, priests and those actively engaged in one religious duty or the other are regarded as ministry professionals. What is given to the sick person at the moment determines who is God-sent. God uses whomever he chooses to execute his mandate in the world. This is not to derogate the function of ordained ministers;

iv. In the works of Rogers and Sullivan, which we examined extensively in this book, there are certain values that everybody should always aspire for and these are the values of interpersonal relations and values of right choices. Choices are fundamental to life, even when we decide not to choose, that is also a choice. There are so many choices in life, but to make the right ones is wisdom;

v. Nobody is an island unto himself. Humanity is interconnected in one-way or the other. Race, language, color or gender has no role or place in God's arithmetic;

vi. Children should always endeavor to respect their seniors, particularly the aged. Of course, respect is reciprocal;

vii. The individual person should be approached as a whole, treated for who he is and not as a piece of wood;

viii. Modern psychiatry and psychoanalysis should take the convenience of the client first before their personal conveniences;

ix. According to Rogers and Sullivan, hard work and determination are the keys to success;

x.   From this study, we gathered that even when one has no religion, there is still the need to focus on something as the source of one's vitality and being. There are so many advantages one could derive from this book, but from our limitations, more work should be done on this open-ended topic and area of study;

xi.   There is need to respect the dignity of the human person, environments, spirituality and bioethics;

xii.   No person is completely useless" (Nwachukwu, O. Anthony, p. xxviii), even the criminal in a prison can change tomorrow. Restorative justice is important. There is need to give offenders and victims the chance to meet and talk. It is unnatural for a person to act like an animal without a reason;

xiii.   Regard people and treat them for who they are and not by the judgments we set about them. We may be shortsighted to see their goodness and this fact becomes a big lesson for me in my nursing profession;

xiv.   There is joy in loving. Love others whether they love back or not, for that is the ideal thing to do. The shortest way to peace is being peaceful;

xv.   Religion should not be practiced to avert punishment by the Church/God; but intrinsically welcomed for the glories it promises;

xvi.   Ritualism and doctrines are not the bases for faith or religious practice but good work energized by faith;

xvii.   Individuals' potentials should be put in full use and not be allowed to rot away. For each person as such, is accountable for his or her success in life;

xviii.   Self-confidence, optimism, determination and reliance are the major keys to science/success;

xix. Nobody is an island unto himself. We need to understand that without interpersonal relations, life may become frustrating and unacceptable;

xx. Sullivan experienced the loneliness of family background and moved from its excruciating agony, hence advocates for interpersonal connectedness;

xxi. Sullivan equally highlighted the importance of religion in a practical fashion. He was not known as one who practiced religion. But he knew it was necessary to belong to one and therefore made a will to be buried as Catholic;

xxii. Human interactions and behaviors should be traced from various sources, genes, parents, associations, environment and one's culture;

xxiii. Life is empty without some sort of relationships because knowing people and their stuffs are the fundamental bases of strong relationships;

xxiv. Every life is as important as the other and to be a superman can be fun. The Pursuit for satisfaction and security is paramount in life and should be the responsibility of every person;

xxv. Education depends more on hard work and focus than family background;

xxvi. Reinforcement brings about motivation and should be encouraged in both high and tertiary institutions;

xxvii. Psychiatry should include psychology and counseling because the manner in which any psychic person is approached affects the healing process, either for good or worse;

xxviii. Psychiatry should involve the treatment of the whole person, applying therapeutic resources as families and friends;

xxix. As against Freud, Sullivan recommends that personality development should not be limited to sexual orientations but to the entire personality;

xxx.   With Sullivan's positions today, I am highly invigorated to find ways to assist people with variety of family problems;

xxxi.   Relationships should not be transference or professional. We relate as human beings by being sensitive to one another's needs. This is the height and apogee of this book because mentalist-based knowledge of psychology is not always the best of it. Counseling should be practical by assisting those in various plights come to grip with the reality of life itself.

C. Recommendations

These are based on related areas other Prospective Researchers can lay their emphases. For instance, they should consult such pieces of work by these renowned authors and experts on psychology and its application to human life, including: John Morgan, the father of modern academician of today, Sigmund Freud, Erik Erikson, Carl Rogers, Harry Sullivan, Alfred Adler etc. The work of Dr. Nwachukwu on spiritual psychology has much to say about psychological practice and value of psychology in human life. There are so many works on psychology both on basic level and the level of application. Academic honesty is important, whereby, the researcher acknowledges the sources he or she has cited and applied to achieve a name. Lots of people have studied one course or the other, and bagged one PhD or the other; yet, the problems in society appear unbendingly unsolved. Therefore, I want to make myself available to assist others through a professional process. For instance, any studies that have no relevance or positive change to the manner and ways people live their daily lives have to be discouraged. As a trained and registered nurse; it is my responsibility to take proper care of my family, friends and others who may approach me for their counseling needs.

On the same par, further studies should be carried out on human interpersonal relationships as to address the reasons for so many divisions we have in society today. Education, both formal and informal should be made affordable to society, particularly by the government. The need for and importance of just distribution of economic resources, which have been affected due to the dwarfism of few individuals, have to be encouraged. The gap between the rich and the poor appears to be increasing on a geometrical rate and it may lead to societal annihilation. While the rich grow richer the poor seem marginalized and debilitated. Psychological practice is the synthesis of any anthropological goal.

The good that is accomplished in human life is better than silver and gold or all other scientific preoccupations that destroy lives. Studies should be carried out on the need for psychological practice from other perspectives other than pastoral as noted already, political, social, and religious, etc. Once the human society is organized holistically to benefit everybody, the individual person will have wide horizons to strive and survive. Therefore, this book has challenged prospective candidates on the study of psychology to deepen their search on variety of areas that impact positively to the advancement of the individual person. Based on the universal academic target of this book, we are bound to state the source of our thesis or bibliography.

CHAPTER SEVEN

BIBLIOGRAPHY

Abbott, Stephanie; Ronsheim, Douglas; Xander, Donna (June 2005). "Counselors and Clergy: Partners in Healing". *Counselor: Magazine for Addiction Professionals*. ISSN 1047-7314. http://www.counselormagazine.com/feature-articles-mainmenu-63/30-spirituality/73-counselors-and-clergy-partners-in-healing. Retrieved 2010-09-15.

Adler, Alfred. 1994. The Drive for Self: Alfred Adler and the Founding of Individual Psychology by Edward Hoffman. NY: Addison-Wesley Publishing.

Alexander, J. (ed). 1966. *The Jerusalem Bible*. Darton: Longman & Todd Ltd.

American Association of Pastoral Counselors/History

Anscombe, G.C.M. 1958. *Intention*. Oxford: Blackwell.

Augsburger, David W. (1989). "Pastoral Counseling". Global Anabaptist Mennonite Encyclopedia Online. http://www.gameo.org/encyclopedia/contents/P381ME.html. Retrieved 2010-09-15.

Baunoch, Joseph (ed). 2006. *Foundation Theology 2006.* South Bend, Indiana: Cloverdale Book Publishers.

Benner, D. G. (2003). *Strategic Pastoral Counseling. Second Edition.* Grand Rapids, Michigan. Baker Academics.

Berkeley, G. 1975. *The Principles of Human Knowledge.* Warnock, C. J. (ed). London: William Collins & Sons Ltd.

Buice, Allison (June 27, 1987). "Pastoral Counselors Increasing in Numbers". Spartanburg Herald-Journal (Spartanburg , SC): p. B3.

Coffey, F. James. 1993. *Seeing With The Heart.* New York: Healy's Graphic Ark Publishers.

Colman, Andrew M. 2003. Oxford Dictionary of Psychology. New York: Oxford University Press.

Corey, S. M. & Corey G. (2006). *Groups: Process and Practice. Seventh Edition.* U.S.A: Thomson Books/Cole.

Donceel, J.F. 1961. *Philosophical Psychology.* London: Sheed & Ward, Inc.

Doniger, Simon (ed). 1967. *Pastoral Psychology.* NY: Meredith Publishers.

Erik, H. Erikson. 1980. *Identity and the Life Cycle.* New York: W.W. Norton & Company.

Flannery, B. Raymond. 1995. *Post-Traumatic Stress Disorder: The Victim's Guide to Healing and Recovery.* New York: The Crossroad Publishing Company.

Frankl, Viktor. Psychotherapy and Existentialism. Selected Papers on Logotherapy. New York: Simon & Schuster.

Freud, Sigmund. 1988: A Life for Our Time by Peter Gay. NY: W. W. Norton & Company.

-------------------- 1901. The Psychopathology of Everyday Life (Zur Psychopathologie des Alltagslebens).

Friedman, J. Lawrence. 1999. Identity's Architect: A Biography of Erik H. Erikson. Cambridge: Harvard University Press.

Gay, Peter. 1988. Freud: A Life for Our Time. NY: W.W. Norton & Company.

Gill, J. James & Co. Eds. 1990. *Human Development: The Jesuit Educational Center for Human Development. Vol. Eleven. No. 3.* NJ: The Jesuit Educational Center.

Goldbloom, D.S. (2006). *Psychiatric Clinical Skills.* Elsevier: Mosby, Inc.

Hall, Todd W. & McMinn, Mark R. (eds). 2000. *The Journal of Psychology and Theology.* California: Rosemead School of Psychology.

Hall, Todd W. & McMinn, Mark R. (eds). 2002. *The Journal of Psychology and Theology.* California: Rosemead School of Psychology.

Hill, C.E. (2004). *Helping Skills: Facilitating Exploration, Insight, and Action. Second Edition.* Washington, D.C: American Psychological Association.

Hoffman, Edward. 1994. The Drive for Self: Alfred Adler and the Founding of Individual Psychology. NY: Addison – Wesley Publishing.

Hoffman, Edward. 1988. The Right to Human: A Biography of Abraham Maslow. Los Angeles: JeremyP. Tarcher, Inc.

Hunter, R.J. (2005). "Pastoral Counseling". *Dictionary of Pastoral Care and Counseling*. Nashville: Abingdon Press. ISBN 068710761X.

Hybels, Bill. 1966. *EVANGELISM: Becoming Stronger Salt and Brighter Light.* Michigan: Zondervan Publishing House.

Josef, Pieper. 1965. *The Four Cardinal Virtues; Prudence, Justice, Fortitude, Temperance,* (tr. Richard & Clara Winston), NY: Harcourt, Brace, and World.

Jung Gustav, Carl. 1940. The Integration of the Personality. London: Routledge and Kegan Paul.

----------------------- 1933. Modern Man in Search of a Soul. London: Kegan Paul Trench Trubner, (1955 ed. Harvest Books)

Keating, Thomas. 2000. The Transformation of Suffering Reflection on September 11 and the Wedding Feast at Cana in Galilee. NY: Lantem Books.

Kilgard, E. R. & Atkinson, R.C. 1967. *Introduction to Psychology 4th Edition.* New York:: Harcourt, Brace & Word, Inc.

Kirschenbaum, Howard. 1979. On Becoming Carl Rogers. NY: Delacorte Press.

Klingberg, Haddon. 2001. When Life Calls Out to Us: The Love and Lifework Of Viktor and Elly Frankl. Jr. NY: Doubleday.

MacNutt, Francis. 1992. *The Power to Heal.* Indiana: Ave Maria Press.

Maslow, Abraham. 2002. The Psychology of Science: Reconnaisance. New York: Harper & Row, Chapel Hill: Maurice Bassett.

------------------------- 1964. Religions, Values and Peak-experiences, Columbus, Ohio: Ohio State University press.

McKenzie, J. L. 1966. *Dictionary of the Bible.* London: Cassoll & Co. Ltd.

McLynn, Frank. 1996. Carl Gustav Jung. NY: St. Martin's Griffin.

Miller, R. W. & Jackson, A. K. (1995). *Practical Psychology for Pastors.* Prentice- Hall, Inc.

Morgan, John H. 2010, Beginning with Freud: The Classical Schools of Psychotherapy. Oh: Wyndham Hall Press

------------------------- (Ed.) 2009. *Foundation Theology 2009 Student Essays for Ministry Professionals.* Mishawaka, Indiana: The Victoria Press.

Morgan, John H. & Neitzke, Russell. 2007. *From Beginning to End. Internet Research and the Writing Process: An author's guide with CD-Rom.* South Bend, IN: Clover Books.

Morgan, John H. 2006. "Being Human and Being Good: The Psychodynamics of Personhood" (Co-ed). *Religion and Society. Summer Programme in Theology 2006.* Indiana: Cloverdale Corporation.

------------------------- 2003. *Unfinished Business. The Terminal All-But-Dissertation Phenomenon in American Higher Education.* Bristol Indiana: Cloverdale Corporation.

Nwachukwu, F.J. & Ugwuegbulam, C. N. 1966. *Guidance and Counselling: An Introductory Survey.* Benin: Barloz Publishers, Inc.

Nwachukwu, Anthony O. 2010. Keeping Human Relationships Together: Self Guide to Healthy Living [Studies in Spiritual Psychology vis-à-vis Human Values]. Indiana: iUniverse Publishers.

Paul, Pamela (May 2005). "With God as My Shrink". *Psychology Today.*

Restak, Richard. 1991. *The Brain Has a Mind of Its Own. Insights from a Practicing Neurologist.* New York: Harmony Books.

Rogers, Carl. 1980. A Way of Being. Boston: Houghton Mifflin Publishers.

---------------------- 1970. On Encounter Groups. New York: Harper and Row Publishers.

---------------------- 1942. Counseling and Psychotherapy: Newer Concepts in practice.

Romero, Anna A. & Kemp, Steven M. 2007. *Psychology Demystified, A Self- Teaching Guide.* New York, NY: McGraw-Hill.

Shlemon, Leahy Barbara. 1982. *Healing The Hidden Self.* Notre Dame, IN: Ave Maria Press.

Stokes, Rodney (1974). "Survey Graphic". reprinted online at the Canadian Association for Pastoral Education and Practice website

Sue, W. Derald & Sue David. 1990. *Counseling the Culturally Different: Theory & Practice (Second Edition).* New York: A Wiley-Interscience Publication.

Sullivan, Harry. Stack. 1953. The Interpersonal Theory of Psychiatry, NY: W.W. Norton & Co.

-------------------------------- 1972. Personal Psychopathology. NY: Norton & Co.

-------------------------------- 1956. Clinical Studies in Psychiatry, Norton & Co.

Webster, M. 1979. *Webster's New Collegiate Dictionary.* Massachusetts: G. & C. Merriam Company.

Wiener, Norbert. 1950. *The Human Use of Human Beings.* New York: Doubleday & Company, INC.

Wolman, B. B. (ed).1973. *Dictionary of Behavioral Science.* New York: Litlon Educational Publishers.

http://www.psychologytoday.com/articles/200505/god-my-shrink. Retrieved 2010-09-18.

http://news.google.com/newspapers?id=iLAeAAAAIBAJ&sjid=jc4 EAAAAIBAJ&pg=5118%2C3469279. Retrieved 2010-10-12.

CHAPTER EIGHT

GLOSSARY OF TERMS AND APPENDIX

A. GLOSSARY

These are some abbreviations and words used in the course of writing that may constitute obstacles to readers. Thus, in the glossary, they are explained such as:

ADHD   Attention Deficits Hyperactivity Disorder – a type of personality disorder

Directee   Refers to the one being directed in spiritual direction

APPC   American Association of Pastoral Counselors

Liminal stage   The action in its full process and completion or the reality stage

Ab initio   From the beginning or start (Latin)

Counselee   The person being counseled

Y.M.C.A   Young Men's Christian Association

W.S.C.F.C   World Student Christian Federation's Conference

Op. Cit.   Opus Citatum (From the work cited – Latin expression)

Ibid   Ibidem – the same place as cited (Latin)

Diakonos   Greek word for deacon

Moralitas   Latin word for Morality

Ad rem   A Latin expression for 'properly suited" or to be applied here

TAMAP   Trained and Approved Medication Administration Personnel

Ipso Facto   By that very fact (Latin)

B. APPENDIX

Appendix 1: My Conversation with the Patient

M = patient (Mary AB), N = Nurse (Myself)

N1 Hello M, I hope you are doing okay

M1 So-so my friend, I can't complain

N2 I am Christy, one of the nurses in this hospital, you have seen me before

M2 Yes Christy, you were here yesterday, am I right, thanks so much for coming to visit me (*smiling*). My husband is sick at home and my two kids don't live around us. I am alone here, as it were.

N3 That sounds so frustrating that you are here alone.

M3 It is. You can't believe the nature of pains I experience on my back because of my spinal dislocation. If you watch me, I cannot sit but simply lie on my back. I strongly believe that the omnipotent God will see me through.

N4 Mrs. M, why can't your children come here to visit you since they are grown-ups. Though you don't look sick except that you are in the hospital

M 4 Christy, my appearance is deceptive; I am in a great pain for quite a long period of time now. I have had this awful back pain for some years now I have gone through one surgery to another surgery. I have had seven surgeries in four years and my situation is not getting any better. Christy, I am tired of staying here. I want to get out of here. I have been here for almost eight months, in and out of the hospital. I want to go home and take care of my husband who is very sick for many years now. I miss him; he cannot come here and there is no way anybody could bring him down to see me. I was a registered nurse and used to take care of him. Sickness has forced me to retire and now I can't do much for him. I really want to go home. My beautiful children have visited once and they call me on the phone most often. You know how our system works here. They are all working. I miss them too *(at this time, patient who has maintained a smiling face as she narrated her stories, began frowning).*

N5 You are really going through a lot. Sorry to hear all that. I know you love your family, should you go home under pains?

M5 I have missed my family so much. Imagine I have been in this hospital almost one year now. Eight months are not eight days. I hear there are chaplains in this hospital; I have only seen one on two different occasions. The doctors, nurses and my physical therapists are always here. I don't like complaining. I am tired of staying here. I watch the Mass at the TV (pointing to the hanging Television in her room). Do you still want to hear more *(laughing aloud)*? *[The Conversation is already contained in the text].*

AUTHOR'S BIOGRAPHY

Christiana Chinedum Onu is the seventh child of the ten children of Late Sir/Chief Celestine Uwazie Onuoha Ekeh (Knight of St. John), and lady Regina Adaku Ekeh.

She attended Teachers College Ehime Mbano, Federal College of Education Abeokuta, and University of Jos, Nigeria. Some of her qualifications include, Teachers Grade Two Certificate, Nigerian Certificate in Education (NCE), Accounting/Office Administration.

She worked in the Ministry of Education Owerri, Imo State, as a Teacher and Primary School Management Board, Local Education Authority, Garki, Abuja as a Statistician. She was the managing Director, Nedueke Nigeria Enterprises Federal Ministry of External Affairs Secretariat, Gariki Abuja, Supplies Division and the Proprietor, of Blessed Pharmacy Philadelphia, PA, USA.

Education is the goal of her family. Here in the States, she had her Associate Degree at Pennsylvania State University, Abington and Bachelor of Science in Nursing (BSN) at LaSalle University Philadelphia, PA. She is currently working at North Philadelphia Health System, ST. Joseph's Hospital Philadelphia as a Staff Nurse. She is a member of the United Nurses of Pennsylvania (UNOP).

Her parents were so generous to a fault. Consequently, she took interest in assisting others. Hence her passions for counseling psychology grew strength to strength. She had her Master's Degree in Pastoral Counseling at Graduate Theology Foundation, Indiana University, Affiliated Institute of Oxford University, England. As scholar of worth, she graduated with an Academic Award, "Mother Teresa's Spirituality and Community Service" partly with scholarship towards her PhD Program. Thanks to God, after her Masters at GTF, her profile was posted in the School Website, an opportunity and prestigious position which not many of her students have ever enjoyed.

Ever since she started her education with GTF, she has come to realize that society needs Counseling Psychology more than any other discipline she ever imagined. Therefore, she applied for admission to pursue her PhD in Counseling Psychology at the same Institution, for which this biography was necessitated. She completed her PhD Program within a record time from the same Institution, not only with flying colors but with First Class Position (Summa Cum Laude) in her PhD academic Defense, in 2012. Thanks to the Almighty God who He has always stood with her in navigating through the uncertainties of life with great success.

Dr. Christiana Chinedum Onu (Nee Ekeh), RN, BSN, MA, PhD

Email address: Christy Onu chimnedum@rocketmail.com

Student Profile @ www.gtfeducation.org

Christyonu1164@gmail.com

Printed in the United States
by Baker & Taylor Publisher Services